Cash Management

Cash Management

A Financial Overview for School Administrators

Enid Beverley Jones

scarecrow
education

The Scarecrow Press, Inc.
A Scarecrow Education Book
Lanham, Maryland, and London
2001

SCARECROW PRESS, INC.
A Scarecrow Education Book

Published in the United States of America
by Scarecrow Press, Inc.
4720 Boston Way
Lanham, Maryland 20706
www.scarecroweducation.com

4 Pleydell Gardens, Folkestone
Kent CT20 2DN, England

British Library Cataloguing-in-Publication Information Available

Library of Congress Cataloging-in-Publication Data

Jones, Enid B.
　　Cash management : a financial overview for school administrators / Enid Beverley Jones.
　　　　p. cm. — (A Scarecrow education book)
　　Includes bibliographical references and index.
　　ISBN 0-8108-4067-7 (pbk. : alk. paper)
　　　　1. Education—United States—Finance. I. Title. II. Series.

　LB2825 .J64 2001
　371.2'06'0973—dc21

2001031076

Contents

Tables

Foreword

In the mid-1990s, the concept of the series *Educational Leadership for the 21st Century* was conceived with the premise that public school systems needed reform. The target population for the series was school administrators who needed to become scholarly practitioners for the twenty-first century and who could demonstrate deliberative responses to the cultural demands placed on education. The series of books dealt with leadership, organization, diversity, and support services. The authors in the series developed new paradigms for the future that could drive the reform.

We have now entered the new century and we need the fuel to drive the new paradigms. That fuel is money; proper management of the budget is paramount. Dr. Enid Beverley Jones of Fayetteville State University has accepted this challenge with *Cash Management: A Financial Overview for School Administrators*. Several concepts are emphasized. The first one justifies the importance of principals in recognition of the gigantic trend toward decentralization in school management. Another is the emphasis on "human capital," which becomes increasingly important as needs increase and money supplies do not. Dr. Jones also emphasizes the need to have a strong understanding of basic economic theory in order to deliver the best possible services to society through education.

Dr. Jones addresses the need for equity, the importance of the various levels of governance and their proper roles, and the impact of the courts and of the legal connections to school finance. However, important as these mega-issues are, there is still a tremendous need to impart practical budgetary procedures to our scholarly practitioners. The book covers these well, with chapters on budgeting at the school level and financing facilities. Through all of these challenges, Dr. Jones emphasizes the role of the building principals and provides solutions for them in this new century.

I feel this book is the missing link to the other resources for school reform. Dr. Jones has made this book a must-read for all administrators. It should also have great utility in graduate classes where school administrators are educated and trained. I am very pleased with how this book addresses the bottom line; readers will be just as pleased.

Dr. William J. Bailey

Preface

Most politicians have, at one time or another, included education as a
key component of their political campaign for election at the local,
state, and national levels of government. Education and training are as
necessary as the air we breathe, and the financing of education must be
in the forefront of the study of education because policy and procedures
are useless without funds to support implementation. There are numer-
ous definitions of school finance; however, a definition of this important topic really boils down to the study of how to find money to provide the resources needed for educating the people of America at
whatever level. Economists have shown from time to time that the
value of money varies with demand and supply in the same way as any
other good, but the demand for money depends on the demand for the
products or items that money can buy. In fact, if there were other ways
to pay for products, then the demand for money would decline; the issue here is not so much the demand for money but the demand for the
resources needed to provide quality education. The supply of money
and resources becomes fairly complex if public education is seen as another sector of the economy pulling on limited supply. As an industry,
it is competing and affecting the prices of the very resources that are to
be purchased. However, because education is not a simple good and because its supply is regulated by laws, the normal rules of competition
do not apply; the study of school finance must then be done in a semi-
market/semi-government arena.

This book is designed to focus on the study of school finance for
principals operating at the local education level, while recognizing the

importance of understanding the principles behind strategies for implementation of policy at the school level. The enormous need for investment to develop human resources for the survival of the society as well
as to produce the educated individual for the survival of self is discussed. Also discussed are the underlying inequities in the educational
system created by the very method of funding that, in addition, allows
for grossly inadequate provision of educational services.

The drive toward equalization of educational opportunity as played
out in state courts is discussed, as is the rationale for state governments
to establish such elaborate systems of state-aid funding formulas. Also
presented are the day-to-day accounting procedures with which a principal should be familiar, along with the principles showing that expenditures must be applied if local, state, and national goals are to be met
at the school level. The relevance of school reform to the working day
of the principal is addressed, as are the political demands of the person
on the front line of the community. Perhaps the most important principle running throughout the book is the reminder to principals of their
ability to ensure a learning environment for students to succeed and to
provide society with value for the huge investment made to education
and to fulfill the goal of quality education for all.

Acknowledgments

A book is not written without the support of many people. I thank my son, Sean, who helped me with my research and patiently typed some of the chapters; my students, who provided a sounding board for some of my ideas; and my friends Claire Scott and Joseph Johnson for their encouragement. I also thank Dr. William Bailey, who suggested that I write down my ideas and who asked me for the completed work often enough that I sat down and wrote it. Most importantly, I dedicate this book to my parents, Gwendolyn and Frederick.

CHAPTER 1

The Economics of Education

Any act designed to effect a beneficial change in people or allow for more employee productivity is an investment in human capital. Education is such an act. Given today's technological changes, the world's economy has become knowledge driven, rather than resource based. This shift has made human capital, and hence education, one of the leading public policy themes of the next century.

Adam Smith (1937) recognized the importance of investment in human capital as early as the late 1930s. In his introduction to the *Wealth of Nations*, Smith stipulated that the keys to a nation's wealth are the skill, dexterity, and judgment with which labor is generally applied. Smith went on to analyze the market forces that influence the demand and supply of labor, as well as the circumstances that govern the development of skill, the institutions that facilitate or retard the proper distribution of the labor force, the manner in which people's values help to determine the investments they make in the training of their children, and a great many other aspects of the complex process included in the development and utilization of human resources (Smith 1937). Smith held, first, that economic growth is primarily an effect of the division of labor; second, that dissimilar talents of individuals are acquired rather than natural, for the most part; and third, that the means through which people develop skills are habit, custom, and education. The United States has experienced huge economic growth and a high standard of living over the years, along with access to educational opportunities. Information technology has allowed for tremendous growth in all sectors of the economy while driving down unit cost of production—so much so that individuals who usually operate on the periphery of the labor market can now participate in it, and most are enjoying a higher standard of living. Yet without some defined minimal level of educational qualifications, some individuals are being left out.

Education in this country has been based on the principle of providing greater access for all since the time the common-school philosophy was put into practice. Hanushek (1996) states that historical investment has produced a labor force of unrivaled skill and has contributed to the extraordinary economic growth of the twentieth century, yet there is a steady decline in the proportion of the population that has access to the changing required level of education for full participation in the growth of the society. In other words, the proportion of the population with access to training necessary to acquire the required skills for the workplace and for life has not increased.

HUMAN RESOURCE AS A FACTOR OF PRODUCTION

Although contemporary economists hold that the three main factors or resources of production are land, capital, and labor, with human resources classified as part of labor, they largely ignore the inherent differences within groups of labor. One definition of the factors is land (a resource or factor that includes the land itself, plus minerals found under the soil), capital (a resource encompassing the building, equipment, and other materials used in the production process), and labor (a group resource that includes the physical and mental talents of human beings applied to the production of goods and services) (Wannacott and Wannacott 1979). This concept of factors of production has remained the cornerstone of the theory.

Capital has a unique feature: in order for society to produce capital, there must be a period of abstinence from consumption or a redirection of resources so that capital can be accumulated to produce more consumer goods at a later time. This process of abstinence in the production and accumulation of capital is called *investment*. Although this view of capital development is perennial, the study of labor was not seen in the same light until recently. The resource of labor involves the mental capacity of human beings, and it is now recognized that the greater the training of the mental capacity, the more likely the greater level of efficiency of the resource. It is incumbent for there to be a period of abstinence from use of some resources so that these resources can be invested in human capital—not only to improve production at a later date but also to ensure the intrinsic development of the human resource in and of itself. Human resource is different from the other resources because it is not inanimate, and hence any development or investment should be at least twofold—for economic production and the development of the educated person. Since education in all forms is the means of developing human resources, policymakers in education should therefore plan to invest at both levels.

The concept of human resource has taken hold in the study of production. In fact, human resource is seen as an important entity in the production equation and may well be the entity that makes the difference between normal and supernormal profit. If human resource combined with the other factors of production or resources works well, then it follows that investment to enhance human resources is a natural part of the process of maintaining and improving productivity and economic development. Hunt (1995) makes the points that investment has not generated a level of academic achievement to improve the workforce. In his report on the state of the workforce in the United States, he wrote that

- members of the entering workforce are generally deficient in basic skills in language and in mathematics
- employees ought to have better "learning" or "problem-solving" skills
- new entrants to the workforce lack a number of interpersonal skills, such as being disciplined enough to meet time commitments, motivated to do a better-than-minimally necessary job, able to work with others, and eager to present a good face to the public

DEFINITION OF HUMAN CAPITAL

Any discussion on human capital investment cannot ignore the broader definition eschewed by Shultz (1981). In his definition, Shultz includes a multifaceted approach to human capital development, namely child care, homework experience, the acquisition of information and skills through schooling, and other improvements in health and education. Hornbeck and Salmon (1991), in defining human capital, refer to the acquired skills, knowledge, and abilities of human beings, such that expenditures on improving human capabilities can be thought of as "investments" in human productivity. In 1960, Shultz (1961) argued that the growth in the American economy after World War II could not be attributed just to the traditional elements of land and man-hours worked, but also to the growth that occurred in the skills and abilities of workers, and in the quality of human inputs to the economy. According to Berg (1969), education and other forms of human capital investment increase output in a variety of ways: by generating new ideas and the techniques that can be embodied in production equipment and procedures; by equipping workers to utilize the new production techniques; by improving the links among consumers, workers, and managers; and by extending the useful life of the stock of knowledge and skills that the people embody, as well as in the educated citizenry needed to maintain a democracy. As Smith (1937) points out, wealth need not be interpreted only as economic wealth but also as wealth in the arts and humanities, in family life, and in more esoteric and philosophic elements of life. It is easy, however, to measure wealth in terms of economics, so much of the literature on human capital focuses on workforce development as if the workplace is industrial and support-service oriented. This belief is reflected in the changing school curriculum, where funding for the arts in schools has declined.

A summary of skills deemed necessary for the workforce in the literature on Workforce 2000 can be derived from the following characterization of the workplace of the future:

- the organizationally flatter, leaner, and more aggressive company created through downsizing will remain
- a generation of "intelligent software" is emerging that will allow for greater flexibility at less expense, and will empower employees at the lowest level of an organization to make critical decisions
- smaller entrepreneurial business units both within bigger organizations and without, as stand-alone units, will prevail

- information sharing will provide instantaneous feedback on performance, opportunities for behavior modification, and identification of new avenues in the organization
- teamwork and peer relationships will be the key in creating value in the organization
- employees will have to become self-directed and self-controlling
- superior products and superior customer service will be needed to compete globally
- companies will adopt a "pay for knowledge" system; that is, a reward for continuous learning and flexibility
- the ability to analyze data, draw conclusions, present recommendations, and offer some degree of computer literacy in the new generation of technology, or at least knowledge of rudimentary statistics (for business), will be critical for advancement or even survival (Berg 1969; Boyette and Conn 1991)

This new role for employees will exert enormous pressure on employees and companies alike to invest in education and training (Boyette and Conn 1991). In the report "Workforce 2000: Key Trends" (1998), the point was made that the new jobs in service industries will demand much higher skill levels than the jobs of the 1990s. Very few new jobs will be created for those who cannot read, follow directions, and use mathematics. Stewart (1997) quotes Shiller of Yale University in saying that 72.1 percent of U.S. households' wealth consists of human capital, where wealth is defined as the present value of expected lifetime wages. Human capital theory suggests that education is a normal good; that is, as income rises, desired education expenditure also rises.

HUMAN CAPITAL AS A PUBLIC GOOD

The American economy is neocapitalist with imperfect markets, rather than the perfect market envisaged by Smith (1937). If market conditions were perfect, then the development of human capital might well be a private matter; given market imperfections, for example, it is impractical for any one employer to bear the cost of training. Information gaps in the market allow neither students nor their parents to have full knowledge of the kinds of training necessary for the job market; thus underinvestment or unwise investment in human capital occurs. Of course, another complicating factor is the lack of funds available to individuals and families for training and education. Human capital is not the same as other tangible assets that can be used as collateral for loans to develop the asset; hence, the credit market is not as open to financing early education. There is no guarantee that acquired skills will be used productively; that is, education is a high-risk investment (Hornbeck and Salmon 1991). Furthermore, the cost is difficult to assess—both actual and opportunity costs—as is the return on the investment. In fact, the productivity of a given quantity of human capital can vary greatly, depending on the individual's decision on use of skills (Parnes 1984). Thus, human capital development remains a public good supported by governmental agencies.

According to Candoli, Hack, and Ray (1992), information has become the source of three-fourths of value added in manufacturing, as manufacturing is dematerializing and pure information is being sought. Even money has become an image of ones and zeros piped through miles of wire, pumped over fiber-optic highways, bounced off satellites, and beamed from one microwave relay station to another. Knowledge has become the most important component of business activity in the emergence of the information age—the economy of intangibles. This is not to say that knowledge has not always been important, but now the value of the stock of intellectual capital has increased in the midst of the economic revolution that is creating the information age. Knowledge has been the preeminent economic resource—more important than raw material, more important than money. Considered as an economic output, information and knowledge are more important than any of the products of the industrial age (Stewart 1997). A case in point is the high value of shares in the on-line company Amazon Books in 1998–1999, even though the company had not reported a profit since inception. Any product that is as important to an economy as human capital has historically been treated as a public good.

Kofi Annan (March 9, 2000), secretary-general of the United Nations, stated that education is an investment that yields a higher profit than any other. If competitive success is achieved through people, and

Table 1.1 Median annual income of year-round, full-time workers, 25 years and over, by educational level (in current dollars)

Sex and year	Less than 9th grade	9th to 12th grade, no HS diploma	High school graduate	Some college	Associate degree	Bachelor's degree
Men						
1991	17,623	21,402	26,779	31,663	33,817	40,906
1992	17,294	21,247	27,280	32,103	33,433	41,355
1993	16,863	21,562	27,370	32,077	33,690	42,757
1994	17,532	22,048	28,037	32,237	35,794	43,663
1995	18,354	22,185	29,510	33,883	35,201	45,266
1996	17,962	22,717	30,709	34,845	37,131	45,846
1997	19,291	24,726	31,215	35,945	38,022	48,616
1998	19,380	23,958	31,477	36,934	40,274	51,405
Women						
1991	12,066	14,455	18,836	22,143	25,000	29,079
1992	12,958	14.559	19,427	23,157	25,624	30,326
1993	12,415	15,386	19,963	23,056	25,883	31,197
1994	12,430	15,133	20,373	23,514	25,940	31,741
1995	13,577	15,825	20,463	23,997	27,311	32,051
1996	14,414	16,953	21,175	25,167	28,083	33,525
1997	14,161	16,697	22,067	26,635	28,812	35,379
1998	14,467	16,482	22,780	27,420	29,924	36,559

Source: Digest of Education Statistics 2000

if the workforce is indeed an increasingly important source of competitive advantage, then it is important to build a workforce that has the ability to achieve competitive success and one that cannot be readily duplicated by others (Pfeiffer 1994). Differences in income reported by the National Center for Education Statistics are set out in table 1.1.

As the median income in table 1.1 shows, the differences in income vary directly with the level of education for both men and women, although women are earning less than men at each level.

COST OF NONEDUCATION

Table 1.1 also demonstrates the impact of noneducation and undereducation, not only in the differences in income but in the accumulation of wealth and the socioeconomic divisions in the nation. In the United States, the assets of the wealthiest 1 percent of the population have grown as the population below the poverty line has swollen (ILO 1995).

In 1994, U.S. Labor Secretary Reich made the point that

We have the most unequal distribution of income of any nation in the world. . . . Unless we turn this situation around, we're going to have a two-tiered society. We can't be a prosperous or stable society with huge gaps between the rich and everyone else. As the economy grows people who work with machines and clean offices and provide the basic goods and services are supposed to share in the gains, but this hasn't been happening. (Reich 1995)

Reich (2000) wrote that hourly and salaried workers are still with us but more of their pay depends on how hard and how well they work. He also points out that disparities in income and wealth have widened considerably and that America is tolerating this high degree of inequality.

Economists maintain that the inequality gap can lower growth in the gross domestic product as overall efficiency is lowered (Romer 1994). In examining the information in table 1.2 on the mean income received by each fifth and the top 5 percent of households, it can be seen that income is indeed unevenly distributed; the lowest fifth receives 12 percent of the income of the top 5 percent, at the upper limits of income. The point is that individuals with marketable skills gained through education can hope to participate in the system with income levels in the higher fifths whereas those without cannot, unless they get a windfall.

In addition to the inability of the lowest fifth of the population to create wealth, the other social and economic costs of not sufficiently educating all citizens can be high. High levels of illiteracy, unemployment, military service incapability, high health costs, expensive public relief budgets, overall lower standards of living, and the reduced quality of life that can be associated with undereducation can result (Bur-

Table 1.2 Income limits for each fifth and top five percent of households (current dollars)

Income level	1999	1998	1997
lower limit of top 5%	142,021	132,199	126,550
fourth-lowest fifth	79,375	75,000	71,500
third-lowest fifth	50,520	48,337	46,000
second-lowest fifth	32,000	30,408	29,200
lowest fifth	17,196	16,116	15,400

Source: United States Census Bureau 1998 [http://www.census.gov]

rup, Brimley, and Garfield 1996). Hodgkinson's (1985) view of the issue is: where there is a high percentage of high school graduates, states get a net gain in the graduates' ability to repay the cost of their education. The reverse is also true, in that a net loss occurs in states with lower graduation rates. Furthermore, there is the unique cost of under-educating the students with special needs.

Illiteracy and Unemployment

The National Center for Education Statistics (NCES 2000) reported that a 1992 assessment of literacy skills for adults found that approximately 22 percent of the adult population lacked the ability to perform simple arithmetic operations, and 21 percent could not locate a simple piece of information in a short text excerpt. Only about one-fifth of the population could solve mathematical problems requiring two or more steps or the integration of information from complex passages. As is well known, illiteracy undermines the quality of life in a society. In keeping with unemployment and illiteracy rates, there are increases in dependency on public relief by the group in society who does not have adequate marketable skills to earn livable wages and salaries. About half of all welfare mothers never finished high school. The recipients of welfare are generally poorly educated (U.S. Bureau of the Census 1998).

The National Center for Education Statistics (1997) also reported that 87 percent of 1992–1993 bachelor-degree recipients were employed, 6 percent were neither employed nor enrolled in college, and 7 percent were enrolled for further education with no employment. Eighty-one percent of noncompletes and associate's degree or certificate recipients were employed in April 1984; the rest were unemployed. The implication here is that elementary and secondary schools should be providing the necessary infrastructure for students to aim for and receive postsecondary education to survive in the job market, and not spend much of their working life unemployed or underemployed. The role of the school principal as the site administrator is defined here as providing these necessary services, with the knowledge that resources will be a constraint but cannot be a limitation in achieving all the equity, adequacy, and equal opportunity goals set for students in the

Table 1.3 Average number of unemployment spells since age 18, by age and educational attainment, 1978–1990

Worker characteristics/age	18	21	24	27
No high school diploma	2.5	4.7	5.9	6.2
High school graduate	1.9	3.4	4.4	4.5
Some college courses	1.8	3.2	4.0	4.0
College graduate	1.4	2.6	3.5	3.7

Source: Venn & Weiss 1993

United States. The rest of this book provides a view for the principal in the school-finance arena.

Venn and Weiss (1993) provided data from the average unemployment spells associated with educational attainment. The average number of spells of unemployment varies inversely with the level of educational attainment. The authors found that by age twenty-seven, college graduates experience 3.7 spells of unemployment while high school dropouts averaged 6.2. They also pointed out that a study of the work history of young workers showed that there are significant differences by sex and by race in the number of unemployment spells. However, comparisons by educational levels show that many of the differences become smaller or disappear completely with an increase in educational attainment. Similarly, the U.S. Census Bureau (1999) reports that 8.5 percent of individuals with no high school diploma were unemployed in 1998, 4.8 percent of high school graduates, 3.6 percent with less than a bachelor's degree, and only 1 percent of college graduates—thus bearing out the point that higher levels of educational attainment can make a difference (table 1.3).

Health Costs

The Centers for Disease Control reported in 1995 that people with fewer than twelve years of education are most likely to engage in high-risk behaviors such as smoking, lack of exercise, and poor eating habits (Hosteller 1994). The U.S. Bureau of the Census (1998) also showed that in 1993, for persons eighteen years and older, 178,000,000 of the labor force had coverage under either government or private health insurance. Of this amount, 42 percent had more than one year of college; 39 percent had completed high school, and 19 percent had less than high

Table 1.4 Dynamics of economic well-being: health insurance statistics, 1992 to 1994

Covered by private and government insurance	Persons 18 years and over	Years of school completed		
		Less than high school	High school no college	College 1 yr or more
All persons	178,064,000	35,435,000	67,426,000	75,203,000
28 months employment	131,922,000	23,940,000	48,150,000	59,831,000
Less than 28 months	46,142,000	11,495,000	19,275,000	15,371,000

Source: U.S. Bureau of the Census 1998

school training. Table 1.4 provides more information on the relationship between levels of education and individuals with health coverage.

This information, coupled with the fact that the labor participation rates are 54 percent males between the ages of sixteen and nineteen and 51 percent females between the same ages, gives the impression that many individuals with less than a high school diploma are not covered by health insurance and hence must depend the welfare system. By 1997, 36.9 percent of low-income families were uninsured, while only 8.6 percent of higher income families were in the same situation. In the case of children, 21 percent of low-income families were among the uninsured, compared to 4.9 percent of those from higher income families (Harley and Zuckerman 2000). As Thornley and Williams (1997) remarked, human development needs human beings to be the initiator, the means and the end of the development. Further, for development to occur, the individual must have the capacity to act. The two key elements for developing human capacity are health and education.

CONCLUSION

The concept of investment in human capital is not new but Adam Smith's theory has been given new life. It is now recognized throughout all nations that investment in human capital is a prerequisite and a necessary condition for economic development, as well as to sustain development at any decent standard of living. Nowhere is this clearer than in less-developed countries where the line of demarcation between the wealthy and the poor coincides with the line between the educated and the under- or uneducated. Such lines are drawing closer together in the United States, although the standard of living is generally not as low as in less-developed countries.

In the United States, education has been treated as a "right" for all individuals; for this and other reasons, education has been funded as a public good. However, the quality of education received has differed greatly between individuals, and the results of low levels of educational attainment are seen in the returns on investment by an increasing dependence on social support systems by the less-educated segment of the population. Little emphasis is placed on the intrinsic value of education; instead, the marketable value of skills is used as a measure of the value of the initial investment in elementary and secondary education as the groundwork for preparing for the workforce. Furthermore, the changing workforce seems to be moving faster than the changes in education to prepare workers with new skills. The residual profit from combining the traditional factors of production can be attributed to the investment in human capital and not just to the synergistic effect of combining factors. In the next chapter, the investment in human capital is explored on a less theoretical plane as the adequacy of funding is explored.

SUMMARY

- Investment in human capital has proven to be the most important investment made in the United States over time. Education has made the difference between a productive workforce and a population destined to drain all other resources.
- The skills necessary to maintain the economy have been redefined to meet the changes in society; education can be the vehicle to effect change. The information age or knowledge age has placed knowledge in the position of being a public good because of the degree of importance of the good to society.
- The rewards to an educated society far outweigh the cost of not educating that society, yet the cost of illiteracy, loss of jobs and wages, health, and income support can be quite high.

DISCUSSION ITEMS

1. Explain the theory that education is an investment in human capital.
2. Select your favorite state legislator and make the case to him or her that investment in human capital can only help the state economy and provide improved well-being in the state.
3. Determine the number of individuals on welfare in your locality and speculate on the increase in income and sales tax revenues that could be generated if these individuals had jobs.
4. The economy is doing so well that the number of individuals available for casual labor is low. Students are dropping out of school at a high rate in your community because the opportunities to earn high salaries are many. Develop a program to convince these students that there is more to getting an education than joining the low end of the job market.

CHAPTER 2

Financing Education
Adequately and Equitably

Over ninety years ago, Dewey (1902) wrote, "What the best and wisest parent wants for his own child, that must the community want for all its children. Any other ideal for our schools is narrow and unlovely; acted upon, it destroys our democracy." The goal of adequacy can be achieved when programs and learning opportunities are sufficient for a particular purpose. The determination of that purpose is essentially a public policy decision. For example, for a student with a disability, adequacy might include the provision of an individualized educational program, developed for the student in consultation with parents and a team of professional educators. For school finance purposes, the program must be converted into those human services and materials needed for the desired effect. In this sense, the concept of vertical equity prevails, since unequal per pupil funding is needed to provide an adequate program. Different parties involved in public school delivery of educational services will have different ideas on what would be needed to achieve adequacy. A superintendent's position may well be influenced by whether sufficient funds are available to carry out the educational programs desired by the community; a principal's position can be influenced by whether the salary schedule is competitive enough to attract and retain high-quality teachers and staff; and a teacher's position is likely to be related to salary and classroom materials. Research suggests that the relationship between educational achievement and resources is positive, but there is really no proof that there is a causal relationship between achievement and money. Nonetheless, the research confirms that more students in poor school districts perform at a lower level than those in wealthier districts across the nation.

The business of providing education in public elementary and secondary school is huge. The personnel, materials, and supplies needed to carry out the operations for schools are drawn from many noneducational industries in the country, and perhaps from outside the country. In other words, changes in the funding of education affects the entire economy. In this section, the cost of providing an education will be examined with the intent of determining if provided funds are adequate for achieving the following stated education goals as outlined by the U.S. Department of Education:

- all American children will start school ready to learn
- the high school graduation rate will increase to at least 90 percent
- American students will leave grades four, eight, and twelve having demonstrated competency in challenging subject matter, including English, mathematics, science, history, and geography; and every school in America will ensure that all students learn to use their minds well, so they may be prepared for responsible citizenship, further learning, and productive employment in our modern economy
- U.S. students will be first in the world in science and mathematics achievement
- every adult American will be literate and will possess the knowledge and skills necessary to compete in a global economy and exercise the rights and responsibilities of citizenship
- every school in America will be free of drugs and violence and will offer a disciplined environment conducive to learning (U.S. Department of Education 1990).

These goals were not achieved by the year 2000 as first envisioned, but they are still viable goals and can be used as the standard of measure. These national goals, combined with other federal, state, and local educational goals, have become the basis for funding schools. School financing is a dynamic field that must change in order to provide adequate funding over time in order to fulfill policy. When the term *adequacy* is used in this context, it has to mean providing resources to maintain educational services at some level to meet defined educational policy. It is the level of fiscal support that is controversial. In a given state, an adequate level of support for all school districts could well be that which is achievable by the wealthiest district. In this way, because the wealthiest district is likely to maintain high levels of resources, and be more innovative and challenging (simply because of the availability of resources and possibly smaller class size) than the less-wealthy districts, all would benefit from the fall out. This has not been the case. The term *adequacy* tends to be synonymous with minimum in many state-aid formulas, thus allowing serious underinvestment in education—that is, in human capital.

MONEY AND EDUCATIONAL ADEQUACY

Determining an adequate support level for education has been at the heart of the discussion on school finance in the present time, but the difficulty of determining such a level is also being discussed. Cost has steadily increased as the demand for other social services has proliferated. Thompson, Wood, and Honeyman (1994) point out that the years from 1920 to 1970 proved to be the time for progressive government services, with the initiation of federal income tax, social security, welfare and other assistance programs, state income taxes, and rising sales and use taxes. These events carried heavy costs that competed with finite resources and hence, a growing unease with the increasing costs of education that must be met by state governments as laid out in their constitutions. Some factors that contributed to the increased costs of the changing educational arena over the years are provisions for private schools, busing, new busing safety standards, federal legislation and mandates for bilingual education and students with disabilities (the 1990 Individuals with Disabilities Education Act), mandates for reducing class size, required testing programs, new safety standards, increased accountability requirements, paid police patrols, increased use of technology, litigation, and a general rise in prices for supplies. Of importance is the fact that there is no consensus about which specific factors affect student performance, but there is evidence that some schools are significantly better than others. Hanushek (1996) shares the example of one inner-city school system serving an entirely black population, where good teachers were found to surpass bad teachers by more than a full grade level of student achievement over a single academic year. The point is that schools can generally make improvements in their performance at no additional cost, simply by using existing resources effectively. Although it might be appropriate to increase spending on schools, perhaps the first priority is restructuring how existing resources are being used—especially in educating special-needs students.

According to data from the United States Department of Education, the amount of money and the number of people involved in the school system are enormous, as can be seen in table 2.1.

Enrollment increased 15 percent between 1988 and 1998 overall, and the number of public schools increased by about 6,343 nationwide. Enrollment is projected to rise by 5 percent between 1996 and 2007, as both elementary and secondary enrollments are projected to have steady increases. The number of teachers is clearly expected to rise concomitantly to 2.9 million by 2007—a 10 percent increase. During the 1970s and 1980s, the number of teachers rose even though enrollment decreased during the same period. Given the inverse movement between enrollment and teachers, the pupil–teacher ratio fell from 22.3 in 1970 to 17.9 in 1985. After 1985, the number of pupils per teacher continued downward to 17.2 and dropped further to 16.8 by 1998. That level of pupil–teacher ratio is an acceptable one for most states because research has shown that a low pupil–teacher ratio is conducive to more effective teaching and learning, but the expenditure needed to achieve this goal is enormous.

With this background on pupils and teachers in the public school system, the picture can be expanded by examining the revenues and expenditures needed to keep the system going. Average annual salaries for public school teachers in current dollars increased 40.7 percent between 1988 and 1998, but by only 1.5 percent in constant dollars (using 1996–1997 dollars) between 1986 and 1996. There has actually been a decline in teachers' salaries since 1990, when measured in constant dollars. For the period 1986 to 1996, the average annual earnings of full-time employees in all industries was less than those of teachers, so the amount of money allocated to salaries from state, federal, and local funds was competitive. Expenditures increased 87 percent over the period, but only represented 4.4 percent of the gross domestic product in 1998—up from 4 percent in 1986. Education expenditures rose to an estimated high of $619 billion in

Table 2.1 Selected data on public schools, fall 1989–fall 1998

	1986	1988	1990	1992	1994	1996	1997/1998
Total number of public schools	83,455	83,165	84,853	87,125	86,211	88,223	89,508
Total enrollment (000s)	39,753	40,189	41,216	42,823	44,111	45,229	46,349
Total number of teachers (000s)	2,244	2,323	2,398	2,459	2,552	2,638	2,744
Pupil/teacher ratio	17.7	17.3	17.2	17.4	17.3	17.1	16.8
Average annual salaries of teachers (current dollars)	26,569	29,564	33,084	35,029	36,609	38,509	41,598
Average annual earnings of full-time employees in all industries (current dollars)	22,432	24,502	26,669	29,060	30,582	32,850	n/a
Revenues for public schools (thousands of dollars)	158,534	192,016	223,341	247,626	273,138	305,051	n/a
Total expenditures (thousands of dollars)	175,200	209,377	248,930	274,335	302,366	339,700	n/a
Total expenditures as percent of gross domestic product	4.0	4.1	4.3	4.4	4.4	4.5	n/a

Source: U.S. Department of Education 1999; U.S. Department of Education 2000

the 1998–1999 school year, with elementary and secondary schools spending about 60 percent of the total.

Revenues from federal, state, and local agencies increased by 88.6 percent between 1986 and 1996 in current dollars. The contributions from each government agency went from 6.4 federal, 49.7 state, and 43.9 percent local in 1986 to 6.8, 46.8, and 46.4 percent respectively in 1996. Major changes in proportions contributed by each level of government occurred around the mid-seventies to early eighties, when federal contributions rose from 8.9 to 9.8 and then fell to 7.4 percent, while state contributions rose from 44.4 to 47.6 percent and local contributions fell from 46.7 to 45 percent. The number of principals and other administrators at the local education level and district level also increased over the years, but as the political climate changed, the size of administrative staff varied.

What are the expected outcomes of public education? What return is expected from the outpouring of these funds? Are the schools provided with sufficient funds to give all students equal access and the quality of education to succeed? At issue is the measure of adequacy. Many states have implemented accountability programs for planning and controlling outcomes of schools. NCES reported that by the 1995–1996 school year, thirty-three states used their testing program for school accountability—thus evaluating principals, teachers, and staff through the performance of students on state-mandated tests. In three states, the courts spelled out what adequacy meant.

In New Hampshire, it was determined that the foundation of an adequate education was an education that:

- provides the physical personnel and material resources necessary for children to acquire the skills, knowledge, and values necessary to develop as responsible and productive citizens and to continue formal and informal learning as adults
- recognizes and responds appropriately to conditions that children possess when they enter school that relate to their ability to acquire the skills, knowledge, and values necessary to develop as responsible and productive citizens

- is managed at the local level in such a way that the resources of the school district are effectively organized for the benefit of children's educational achievement
- results in student educational achievement that meets the standards necessary for children to acquire the skills, knowledge, and values necessary to develop as responsible and productive citizens (defined by plaintiffs in *Claremont v. Governor* [635 A.2d 1375, 1993]).

In ruling the finance system unconstitutional, the court stated that the Constitution imposed a duty to provide adequate education and to guarantee adequate funding.

In Kentucky, as a result of *Rose v. Council for Better Education, Inc.* (790 S.W. 2d 391, 1989), the court stated that a constitutionally adequate public education system should include:

- sufficient oral and written communication skills to enable students to function in a complex and rapidly changing civilization
- sufficient knowledge of economic, social, and political systems to enable the student to make informed choices
- sufficient understanding of governmental processes to enable the student to understand the issues that affect his or her mental and physical wellness
- sufficient grounding in the arts to enable each student to appreciate his or her cultural and historical heritage
- sufficient training or preparation or advanced training in either academic or vocational fields so as to enable each child to choose and pursue life work intelligently
- sufficient levels of academic or vocational skills to enable public school students to compete favorably with their counterparts in surrounding states, in academics, or in the job market

In North Carolina, the Supreme Court defined an adequate education in *Leandro v. State of North Carolina* (Supreme Court of North Carolina no. 179PA96, 1997) as a sound, basic education that will provide the student with at least:

- sufficient ability to read, write, and speak the English language, and a sufficient knowledge of fundamental mathematics and physical science to enable the student to function in a complex and rapidly changing society
- sufficient fundamental knowledge of geography, history, and basic economic and political systems to enable the student to make informed choices with regard to issues that affect the student personally or affect the student's community, state, and nation
- sufficient academic and vocational skills to enable the student to successfully engage in postsecondary education or vocational training
- sufficient academic and vocational skills to enable the student to compete on an equal basis with others in further formal education or gainful employment in contemporary society

The court in North Carolina went further to address the issue of preschool education in stating that the state constitution does not limit the right of every child to the opportunity to receive a sound, basic education based on an achieved chronological age, but rather based on the needs of the particular child. In so doing, the court moved the discussion on education finance firmly away from equity issues into the realm of needs and adequacy.

FINANCING EDUCATION EQUITABLY

Defining and measuring equity are not as difficult as defining adequacy in education finance. This is not to say that the concept is fully understood nor is it static; both adequacy and equity must be seen in a dynamic sense if some achievement at both levels is to occur. In fact, it could be said that both can only be achieved given certain assumptions and within a given period of time, after which conditions and changing assumptions must lead to new definitions. Thompson et al. (1994) maintain that if adequacy is the concept of having enough resources to provide for children's educational needs, equity is the concept of a fair and just method of distributing resources among those same children. Implicit in this definition of equity is at least one facet of adequacy: if educational needs are to be a basis for distribution, then resources must be distributed unequally to adequately serve special-needs students as well as regular students. This means spending at least as much on children living in poverty as is spent on those living in wealthier conditions. As Molnar (1995) puts it, to spend enough to buy a Cadillac education for some children while others must settle for a used Chevette is an obvious affront to the constitutional principles. Swanson and King (1997) make the point that determination of adequacy rests on standards of sufficiency and may be unrelated to the standard of equity, as, for example, when schools within a state may provide equitable educational opportunities for students, but they may fall short of a standard of adequacy. Also, resources for educational programs may be declared at least minimally adequate in all schools, but there may be large disparities among districts.

FISCAL NEUTRALITY

The concept of fiscal neutrality cannot be ignored when considering equity. Fiscal neutrality was the basis of the case *Serrano v. Priest* (96 Cal. Rptr.601, 487 P 2d 1241, 5 Cal. 3d 584) in California in 1971, where it was stated that funding for a child's education should not be a function of the wealth of his or her place of residence but rather should be a function of the wealth of the state as a whole (Coons, Clune, and Sugarman 1970)—thus revoking the inherent differences in funding at the district level resulting from an education finance plan based on the property, income, or other measures of the wealth of the school district. Inherently, such differences in wealth will lead to inequities in funding unless artificially corrected. Many states adjusted their state-aid funding formulas in an attempt to arrive at fiscal neutrality but have fallen short of the goal.

VERTICAL EQUITY

Vertical equity, another concept that cannot be ignored, is defined in the literature on education finance as unequal treatment of unequals—providing resources to meet the needs of students with additional needs beyond those of "regular" students. The examples usually given concern the needs of students seen as exceptional, in that they are physically, mentally, or emotionally challenged. However, these needs can also be defined in terms of low socioeconomic issues, urban and rural schools with problems and issues peculiar to their location, and even with safe-school environments. As Hess (1995) points out, the traditional solution to vertical equity concerns has been to establish a set of categorical programs with funding set on the basis of resources to meet each qualifying student's needs. He continues to consider whether these categorical approaches actually provide enough assistance to compensate for the various disadvantages brought to schools with special-needs students. To determine funding for vertical equity, it is necessary to determine if the funding is adequate for providing students with equal educational opportunity, regardless of differences in needs, regardless of whether these needs are physical or derived from socioeconomic or other conditions.

HORIZONTAL EQUITY

Equal treatment of equals is the popular definition of horizontal equity. This definition has been applied in examining distribution of resources to students, teachers, and schools, and in determining fairness in tax burdens (Thompson et al. 1994; Odden and Picus 1992; Alexander and Salmon 1995). In this context, students are the objects of concern. As Odden and Picus state, horizontal equity requires that all students who are assumed equal or homogenous receive equal shares of resources, such as total local and state general revenues, total current operating expenditures, instructional expenditures, and instruction in the intended curriculum.

Typically, these issues are considered at the state level as policy-makers attempt to incorporate the principles in policies, regulations, standards, and practices to be given to the schools. However, even without the strict oversight practiced by governmental agencies, it seems incumbent on principals to ensure the inclusion and achievement of all these principles as they carry out strategies at the school level. After all, even with limited autonomy, the principal as the site administrator has authority and the responsibility to all parties to strive for equity and adequacy for students. Indeed, it is perhaps only the principal—in collaboration with parents, teachers, staff, and students themselves—who can achieve real equity and adequacy, because he or she is at the place where needs can be assessed, measured, and satisfied, or have information collected to be reported for further planning.

CONCLUSION

Inequitable conditions between school districts have created a dual school system similar to the system the colonists tried to avoid when they left the old country. This dual system is more the result of de facto issues than de jure, but the effects and results are the same and the inequities have persisted, even with attempts to correct the problem. This is because of the dependence on local school district wealth as a base for funding schools. Today, the policymakers in education finance are applying adequacy analysis along with equity measures to examine the effectiveness of the state school finance system, in the hope that there will be more acceptable outcomes for the increasing cost of education. Revenues and expenditures for education have increased as the enrollment increases; education as a "business" sector of the economy employs more teachers and workers in general. Yet although revenues and expenditures have continued to rise, education has remained a constant 4 percent of the gross domestic product. The questions remain as to whether the funds are sufficient and whether they are being used efficiently to reduce differences between districts while achieving educational goals. It is clear that the persistent underlying inequities cannot be ignored; as Kozol (1992) puts it, even if the destruction of the democracy were not threatened by savage inequalities in schools, the destruction of individual lives and ideals is certain.

SUMMARY

- The national educational goals that were projected to be achieved by the year 2000 were not realized and this was partly due to the inadequate funding of public schools, despite the increase in spending over time across society. Many of the policies that were implemented were not funded adequately. For example, the Individuals with Disabilities Education Act included mandates for the reduction of class size and increased use of technology but could not be implemented because of a lack of additional funds in many school districts.

- The requirements for adequate schools were spelled out in three states that experienced litigation challenging the school finance system: New Hampshire, Kentucky, and North Carolina.
- Terms such as *fiscal neutrality, vertical and horizontal equity*, and *adequacy* were defined to make the actions of the court clear.

DISCUSSION ITEMS

1. You do not believe that financial inequity is the reason for disparities in school district funding. Rather, you believe there is an underlying problem of inadequate funding across the state. Prepare arguments supporting your view.
2. Your teachers have been using their personal money to purchase supplies for grades K–3 in the elementary school where you are the instructional leader. The teachers have not complained but you recognize the inherent inequity in such a situation. You have joined with other principals in your district who have the same issue and requested a special meeting with the school board to develop strategies to correct the situation. Outline the persuasive arguments you would use to change the situation.
3. You are the principal in a school district that has been recently co-opted into another wealthier district. No attempt has been made to provide resources that would allow your school to be on par with the facilities, materials, and teaching staff at these wealthier schools, yet your school lost the low-wealth supplement it used to receive before the redistricting took place. How can you convince the superintendent of the district to address this issue of inadequate funding that has led to intradistrict inequity?
4. Provide data to show whether there has been increased spending on public education since 1996.
5. Show how changes in population migration to the South have affected the adequacy of funding for public education in southern states.

CHAPTER 3

The Role of State, Local, and Federal Government

The word "education" is conspicuous in its absence from the U.S. Constitution; however, the Tenth Amendment of the Constitution lays the responsibility for children's education squarely at the door of state governments by stating that "[t]he powers not delegated to the United States by the Constitution nor prohibited by it to states are reserved to the states respectively or to the people." The education clauses in each state's constitution support this function of the state governments. Despite this recognition of responsibility, state funding for public schools was not significant until the 1930s. In the fiscal year 1929–1930, states contributed only 16.9 percent of total revenue for public education.

THE ROLE OF THE STATE IN PUBLIC EDUCATION

The responsibility that state governments carry is laid out in the education clause of the state constitutions. These clauses laying out the legal authority and responsibility of state governments:

State Education Clauses

Alabama

It shall be the duty of the Board [of Education] to establish, throughout the State, in each township or other school-district which it may have created, one or more school, at which all the children of the state between the ages of five and twenty-one years may attend free of charge. (Alabama Const. Art. XI, Sec. 6)

Alaska

The legislature shall by general law establish and maintain a system of public schools open to all children of the State and may provide for other public educational institutions. (Alaska Const. Art. VII, Sec. 1)

Arizona

The legislature shall provide for a system of common schools by which a free school shall be established and maintained in every school district for at least six months in each year. (Arizona Const. Art. II, Sec. 6)

Arkansas

State shall ever maintain general, suitable and efficient system of free schools whereby all persons in the state between the ages of six and twenty-six years may receive gratuitous instructions. (Arkansas Const. Art. 14, Sec.1)

California

The legislature shall provide for a system of common schools by which a free school shall be kept up and supported in each district at least six months every year. (California Const. Art. 9, Sec. 1)

Colorado

The general assembly shall, as soon as practicable, provide for the establishment and maintenance of a thorough and uniform system of free public schools throughout the State wherein all residents of the State between the ages of six and twenty-six may be educated gratuitously. (Colorado Const. Art. IX, Sec. 2)

Connecticut

There shall be always free public elementary and secondary schools in the state. (Connecticut Const. Art. B, Sec. 1)

Delaware

The General Assembly shall provide for the establishment and maintenance of a general and efficient system of free public schools, and may require by law that every child, not physically or mentally disabled, shall attend the public schools, unless educated by other means. (Delaware Const. Art. X, Sec. 1)

Florida

Adequate provision shall be made by law for a uniform system of free public schools. (Florida. Const. Art. LX, Sec.1)

Georgia

The provision of an adequate education for the citizens shall be a primary obligation of the State of Georgia, the expense of which shall be provided for by taxation. (Georgia Const. Art. VIII, Sec. 1; Georgia Code Sec. 2-4901)

Hawaii

The State shall provide for the establishment, support and control of a statewide system of public schools free from sectarian control. (Hawaii Const. Art. X, Sec.1)

Idaho

[I]t shall be the duty of the legislature of Idaho to establish then maintain general uniform and thorough system of public, free common schools. (Idaho Const. Art. IX, Sec. 1)

Illinois

A fundamental goal of the people of the state is the educational development of all persons to the limits of their capacities. The state shall provide for an efficient system of high quality public education institutions and services. . . . The state has primary responsibility for financing the system of public education. (Illinois Const. Art. X, Sec. 1)

Indiana

[I]t should be the duty of the General Assembly to encourage, by all suitable means, moral, intellectual, scientific, and agricultural improvement; and provide by law, for a general and uniform system of common schools, wherein tuition shall be without charge, and equally open to all. (Indiana Const. Art. 8, Sec. 1)

Iowa

The Board of Education shall provide for the education of all the youths of the state through a system of common schools and such school shall be organized and kept in each school district at least 3 months of each year. (Iowa Const. Art. IX, Sec. 12)

Kansas

The legislature shall provide for intellectual educational, vocational, and scientific improvement by establishing and maintaining public schools. (Kansas Const. Art. 4, Sec. 1)

Kentucky

To provide an efficient system of common schools throughout the Commonwealth. (Kentucky Const. Sec.183)

Louisiana

The general assembly shall establish free public schools throughout the State. (Louisiana Const. Title VIII, Sec. 136)

Maine

Legislature shall require towns to support public schools . . . and it shall be their duty to require, the several towns to make suitable provision, at their own expense, for the support and maintenance of public schools. (Maine Const. Art. VIII, Sec.1)

Maryland

The General Assembly . . . shall, by law establish throughout the state a thorough and efficient system of free public schools. (Maryland Const. Art. VII, Sec. 1)

Massachusetts

(I)t shall be the duty of legislatures and magistrates, in all future periods of this commonwealth, to cherish the interests of literature and the sciences, and all seminaries of them, . . . public schools and grammar schools in the towns. (Massachusetts Const. Ch. 5, Sec. 2)

Michigan

The legislature shall maintain and support a system of free public elementary and secondary schools as defined by law. (Michigan Const. Art. VIII, Sec. 2)

Minnesota

[I]t is the duty of the legislature to establish a general and uniform system of public schools. (Minnesota Const. Art. XIII, Sec. 1 or Art. VIII, Sec. 3—The legislature . . . will secure a thorough and efficient system of public schools in each township in the State).

Mississippi

[I]t shall be the duty of the legislature to encourage, by all suitable means, the promotion of intellectual, scientific, moral, and agricultural improvement, by establishing a uniform system of free public schools. (Mississippi Const. Art. VIII, Sec. 1)

Missouri

[T]he general assembly shall establish and maintain free public schools for the gratuitous instruction of all persons in this state within ages not in excess of twenty-one years as prescribed by law. (Missouri Const. Art. IX, Sec. 1(a))

Montana

The legislature shall provide a basic system of free quality public elementary and secondary schools. (Montana Const. Art. X, Sec.1)

Nebraska

The Legislature shall provide for the free instruction in the common schools of this State of all persons between the ages of five and twenty-one years. (Nebraska Const. Art. VIII, Sec. 6)

Nevada

The Legislature shall provide for a uniform system of common schools, by which a school shall be established and maintained in each school district at least six months in every year. (Nevada Const. Art. XI, Sec. 2)

New Hampshire

[I]t shall be the duty of the legislators and magistrates, in all future periods of this government to cherish the interest of the literature and the sciences, and all seminaries and public schools. (New Hampshire Const. Art. 33)

New Jersey

The legislature shall provide the maintenance and support of a thorough and efficient system of free public schools. (New Jersey Const. Art. 8, Sec. 4)

New Mexico

A uniform system of free public schools sufficient for the education of, and open to, all the children of school age in the state shall be established and maintained. (New Mexico Const. Art. XII, Sec. 1)

New York

The legislature shall provide for the maintenance and support of a system of free common schools wherein all the children of the state may be educated. (New York Const. Art. II, Sec. 1)

North Carolina

The general assembly . . . shall provide, by taxation and otherwise, for a general and uniform system of public schools, wherein tuition shall be free of charge to all the children of the State. (North Carolina Const. Art. IX, Sec. 2)

North Dakota

[T]he legislative assembly shall make provision for the establishment and maintenance of a system of public schools which shall be open to all children of the State of North Dakota and free from sectarian control. (North Dakota Const. Art. 8, Sec. 147)

Ohio

The general assembly shall make such provisions, by taxation, or otherwise, as with the income arising from the school trust fund, will secure a thorough and efficient system of common schools throughout the state. (Ohio Const. Art. XI, Sec. 2)

Oklahoma

The legislature shall establish and maintain a system of free public schools wherein all children of the state may be educated. (Oklahoma Const. Art. 13, Sec.1)

Oregon

The legislative Assembly shall provide by law for the establishment of a uniform and general system of common schools. (Oregon Const. Art. VIII, Sec. 3)

Pennsylvania

The General Assembly shall provide for the maintenance of a thorough efficient system of public education to serve the needs of the Commonwealth. (Pennsylvania Const. Art. 3, Sec. 4)

Rhode Island

[I]t shall be the duty of the general assembly to promote public schools, and to adopt all means which they may deem necessary and proper to secure to the people the advantages and opportunities of education. (Rhode Island Const. Art. XII, Sec.1)

South Carolina

The General Assembly shall provide for a liberal system of free public schools for all children between the ages of six and twenty-one years. (South Carolina Const. Art. 9, Sec. 3)

South Dakota

It shall be the duty of the legislature to establish and maintain a general and uniform system of public schools wherein tuition shall be without charge, and equally open to all, and to adopt all suitable means to secure the people the advantages and opportunities of education. (South Dakota Const. Art. VIII, Sec. 1)

Tennessee

The General Assembly shall provide for the maintenance, support and eligibility standards of a system of free public schools. (Tennessee Const. Art. II, Sec. 12)

Texas

[I]t shall be the duty of the legislature of the state to establish and make suitable provision for the support and maintenance of an efficient system of public free schools. (Texas Const. Art. VII, Sec. 1)

Utah

The legislature shall provide for the establishment and maintenance of a uniform system of public schools, which shall be open to all the children of the State. (Const. Art. X, Sec. 1)

Vermont

Laws for the encouragement of virtue and prevention of vice and immorality ought to be constantly kept in force, and duly executed, and a competent number of schools ought to be maintained in each town unless the general assembly permits other provisions for the convenient instruction of youth. (Vermont Const. Ch. 11, Sec. 64)

Virginia

The General Assembly shall establish and maintain an efficient system of public free schools throughout the State. (Virginia Const. Art. IX, Sec. 129)

Washington

The legislature shall provide for a general and uniform system of public schools. (Washington Const. Art. IX, Sec. 1)

West Virginia

The legislature shall provide, by general law, for a thorough and efficient system of free schools. (West Virginia Const. Art. XII, Sec. 1)

Wisconsin

The legislature shall provide by law for the establishment of district schools, which shall be as nearly uniform as practicable; and such schools shall be free and without charge for tuition to all children between the ages of 4 and 20 years. (Wisconsin Const. Art. 10, Sec. 3)

Wyoming

The legislature shall provide for the establishment and maintenance of a complete and uniform system of public instruction, embracing free elementary schools of every kind and grade. (Wyoming Const. Art. 7, Sec. 1)

All states and the District of Columbia accepted the responsibility, as can be seen in their contribution to public education. Actual state support for public education ranged from 7.4 percent in New Hampshire to 89.5 percent in Hawaii, as outlined in appendix A. The numbers in the tables in appendix A at best provide a picture in averages. Since both state and federal funds are being distributed according to local ability and willingness to fund public schools in the case of the former, and to provide equal opportunity in the case of the latter, individual districts and even individual schools could receive amounts far in excess of the average amounts and percentages mentioned above. In North Carolina, for example, the proportion of state contribution to school funds has increased to about 70 percent because of supplementary funding programs, such as low-wealth, small, and rural school districts, and special education programs.

The state's role in public education emerged through attempts to resolve equity and fiscal neutrality issues plaguing the school systems. Equalization of state-aid finance plans is the direct result of the attempt to resolve equity issues and meet the long-established standard of fiscal neutrality. Burrup et al. (1996) mention that, in the early part of the nation's history, most of the costs of school operations were defrayed with nonmonetary services. The states' policies on education finance have come a long way since then, as it was recognized that the ability to provide services varied greatly between local communities. In order for the school system to survive the transfer of ability between communities, the state's role was redefined. For states to provide even the minimum educational program within constitutional boundaries, the governments developed "intergovernmental revenue transfer systems to develop state fiscal assistance to the public schools" (173).

STATE-AID FORMULAS

Each of the fifty states has developed equalization plans suited to its philosophy, and it is therefore difficult to classify these plans by state. However, even with this constraint, general classifications emerge from the literature. In table 3.1, the state-aid plans are measured along a continuum stretching from the most equitable to a level of inequity, where equity is really a measure of fiscal neutrality insofar as the equalization plans are designed to reduce the impact of local wealth on school funding. The assumption behind this analysis is that services for students are identical, except in the cases where exception are identified; in that case, the weighted pupil program is applied. Furthermore, funding differences of school districts and variations between districts are ignored or held constant. To give an idea of some of the differences between districts in state funding, a breakdown of per pupil expenditure from the ten wealthiest and the ten poorest school districts in North Carolina,

Table 3.1 State-aid plans

Equalization plans	Description	Level of equity
No state involvement	schools financed by local and private funds only	none
Nonequalization grants	local funding with some funds, which could be categorical or general from state	low, if any
Matching grants	local funding with some funds from state, which must be matched by some local funds, and could be general or categorical	low, if any
Flat grants	fixed amount from state allocated on per pupil basis	low, possibility of some
Minimum foundation programs	funds from state, based on a basic education program with mandated minimum level of local fiscal effort	low, possibility of high
Guaranteed tax yield/percentage	state funds according to a guaranteed state defined local property tax yield per pupil	high
Guaranteed tax base	state funds according to a guaranteed state-defined local property valuation per pupil	high
District power equalization	state equalization plan that includes recapture provision	high
Weighted pupil program	state equalization program that assigns weight according to degree of exceptionality; helps to attain vertical equity	very high
Combination programs	includes the strong equitable points of various programs and foundation programs	very high
Full state funding	complete state funding for all district costs	complete

as measured by ability of local government to fund their schools was selected, and the proportion of state and local funding displayed in appendix B.

In summary, the state-aid equalization formula to determine state contribution to per pupil expenditure for basic education programs could be expressed in one basic equation, as shown in equation 3.1.

Equation 3.1

$$LC = SA - RPPE$$

Where: LC = local contribution,

SA = state aid, and

RPPE = required per pupil expenditure

Local contributions are given significance in this formula, which is unusual but is done here because local funding is very important for the principal; the wealth of the community determines the school facilities and level of local funding for the school. In the early stages of state-funding formulas, there was no required per pupil expenditure, but with the foundation programs forming the basis of hybrid state-equalization formulas, there is a required per pupil amount— usually predetermined by the state. State aid, then, is actually a residual amount after the local contribution is determined by any working formula that can be derived from the basic equation provided above.

Full State Funding

Under full state funding, it is assumed that the state provides the revenues for the school system. Under this model, funds are provided on a per unit basis for each district, where unit can be students, teachers, etc. No excess spending is allowed. Hawaii is the only state where full state funding could be said to exist, with New Mexico, Washington, and Michigan using some hybrid plan that functions as if there were full state funding. As a state-aid formula, it removes the differences in capacity to provide revenues, as well as differences in a tax effort that exists when school district lines are used as a way of defining funding units. In theory, full state funding addresses the issue of fiscal neutrality, thus promoting uniformity in funding across the state in that it removes inequities created by the coincidence of district lines with lines separating neighborhoods. Morrison (1930) maintained that full state funding would satisfy the state's responsibility for education as authorized in the education clauses of state constitutions.

Combination/Tier Programs

Many states combine programs to achieve the desired state-aid plan. The most popular base for combination programs is the foundation program, which, as the name suggests, provides the minimum funding needed to give each student a defined basic education to meet specific goals of the state. For example, the guaranteed tax yield program could be structured to nullify the ability of districts to exceed the minimum foundation program by limiting the district's ability to raise additional funds because there is a higher level of taxing capacity.

Weighted Pupil Program

This program is designed for resources that allow for the types of vertical equity adjustments to school finance formulas. The adjustments reflect legitimate reasons for providing unequal resources to meet unequal needs. The weightings can be in the form of special appropriations or grants and weightings of the individual students in such programs. The actual weight assigned depends on the identified level of exceptionality. The defining of special education categories is difficult and controversial, partly because of built-in problems associated with any form of labeling students. In many states, there is a cap placed on the amount of funds that can be allocated under this weighting program, so that the level of equity can be less than the formula would imply if a pure weighting system were in place.

District Power-Equalizing Plan

The district power-equalizing plan is used to achieve equity by allowing "excess" funds generated by the local districts' tax efforts to be recaptured by the state, which then distributes the funds to less-wealthy districts or holds the funds for distribution at a later time. The term "excess" could be seen as excess over state-defined guaranteed minimum wealth levels above the minimum foundation amount needed for basic education. Local control over spending is maintained by state effort and equity is also at work—that is, negative state aid.

Percentage-Equalizing Plan

Updegraff (1922) saw the power-equalizing plan as a means of fiscal equalization without loss of local control. Under the percentage-equalizing plan, the level of fiscal effort of each school district is equalized as the state establishes the state guarantees to match local districts' spending levels with revenue from state sources—that is, the state matches at a variable ratio depending on district wealth (Jones 1985).

Guaranteed Tax Base (GTB)

The GTB program allows for each local school district to be funded as if there were a constant tax base per unit of tax effort. The goal of this plan is equalization of the tax base so that revenue differences between districts are due to differences in local tax rate, not differences in assessed valuation of property (Jones 1985) The state guarantees that every district has the same amount of funds after the application of the formula.

Guaranteed Tax Yield (GTY)

GTY differs only slightly from GTB in that this program allows for a constant unit yield for each unit of tax effort in the district. As is the case in percentage-equalizing plans, the local district determines the spending level. The desired spending per pupil divided by the state GTB yields the tax rate the district must apply to its property valuation, such that the tax rate equals spending/GTB. State aid is the difference between the amounts that would be raised under GTB and those that are actually raised under the local assessed valuation (AV) of local property.

Minimum Foundation

Foundation programs as espoused by Strayer and Haig (1923) guarantee a minimum unit amount or above with which each school district is funded. This program requires a uniform local tax effort. Under this plan, state government sets minimum local property tax rates and minimum spending levels for local school districts. State aid ensures that both districts tax and spend at the same foundation spending level. Excess spending is usually allowed.

Flat Grant

Funds are distributed by the state regardless of amount raised locally. There is no attempt at equalization.

Nonequalized Grants

Nonequalized grants can be categorical or general grants allocated with specific spending requirements, or without restrains respectively. Some of these grants can be "matching grants" to be funded in part by the local district.

During the school year, the principal must make choices and decisions to ensure that the students are given equal access and opportunity for their education, regardless of the state-aid formula in place. Since the principal has some control over local funds, understanding the philosophy behind the state-aid formula can help in decision making at the local educational level.

Source of Revenue for State Government

Although state revenues are generated from several sources, it is the revenue provided by sales taxes that is most often used for funding schools. General sales tax is used in forty-five states; some states allow local governments to attach some percentage for local revenue. Yield from sales tax is determined by the following formula:

Equation 3.2
$$\text{tax yield} = \text{base} \times \text{rate}$$
where the yield = the return
base = the product or service sold
rate = a predetermined levy set by state government

Clearly, the greater the volume of sales in any given period, the higher the yield, since the rate is a fixed proportion of an increasing base. In order to estimate how successful a tax is going to be, it is essential to evaluate the viability of the tax by applying certain tests. Such tests include estimating the permanency and adequacy of the yield; the size and permanency of the tax base; equity (horizontal and vertical) of the tax in relation to the taxpayer who actually carries the burden of the tax; the benefit, ability to pay, and sacrifice principle; the neutrality of the tax; the economic effects of the tax; and the cost of administration and compliance of the tax. Further, a tax can be seen as progressive or regressive based on the ratio of the tax to the income of the party affected by the tax. The sales tax is considered to be regressive, although it was not designed as such. This is because the sales tax (a tax on consumption) absorbs a higher proportion of the income of low-income families than of wealthier families. State lotteries have become popular as a means of adding to state general funds to enhance expenditure for public services in general, and public education in particular. However, research has shown that state lotteries are regressive in nature, inefficient, and have not produced the increase in revenue that was expected (Clotfelter and Cook 1989).

The illustration in table 3.2 can be used to provide a broad example of the revenue-generation process using different types of state formulas.

Table 3.2 Illustration of funding

Suppose the foundation amount set by a state is $1,500 per pupil and the state requires a minimum tax rate of 15 mills. What will be the local contribution, state contribution, and total spending for each of the following districts, assuming the flat grant, full state funding, and foundation programs were all tried?

	Number of pupils	Assessed real property value	Actual local tax rate
District A	1,000	20,000 per pupil	45 mills
District B	2,000	25,000 per pupil	30 mills
District C	1,500	130,000 per pupil	20 mills

The state was prepared to provide a flat grant amount of $1000.

Solution: Flat Grant

District A

Local contribution:	($20,000 × .045) = $900 per pupil
State contribution:	($1,000)
Per pupil expenditure:	($1,000 + 900) = $1,900
Total expenditure:	($1,900 × 1,000 pupils) = $1,900,000.

District B

Local contribution:	($25,000 × .030) = $750 per pupil
State contribution:	($1,000)
Per pupil expenditure:	($1,000 + 750) = $1,750
Total expenditure:	($1,750 × 2,000 pupils) = $3,500,000.

District C

Local contribution:	($130,000 × .020) = $2,600 per pupil
State contribution:	($1,000)
Per pupil expenditure:	($1,000 + 2,600) = $3,600
Total expenditure:	($2,600 × 1500 pupils) = $5,400,000.

Solution: Full State Funding

Total number of students in the state:	(1000 +2000 +1500) = 4,500 pupils
PPE to be raised from local taxes:	($900 + 750 + 2,600) = $4,250 per pupil
Total from local contribution:	($4,250 × 4,500) = $19,125,000
Total state contribution @ $1,500 PP:	($1,500 × 4,500) = $6,750,000
Per pupil expenditure:	$6,750,000 + 19,125,000)/4,500 pupils OR ($4,250 + 1,500) = $5,750 for each student in the state.

Solution: Foundation Plan

District A

Local contribution required by state:	(20,000 × .015) = $300 per pupil
State contribution:	($1,500 − 300) = $1,200 per pupil
Actual local contribution:	($20,000 × .045) = $900 per pupil
Per pupil expenditure:	(1,200 + 900) = $2,100
Total expenditure:	(2,100 × 1000) = $2,100,000

District B

Local contribution required by state:	($25000 × .015) = $375 per pupil
State contribution:	($1,500 − 375) = $1,125 per pupil
Actual local contribution:	($25,000 × .030) = $750 per pupil
Per pupil expenditure:	($1,125 + 750) = $1,875
Total expenditure:	($1,875 × 2,000) = $3,750,000

District C

Local contribution required by state:	($130,000 × .015) = $1,950 per pupil
State contribution:	($1,500 - 1,950) = -$450 per pupil OR zero
Actual local contribution:	($130,000 × .020) = $2,600 per pupil
Per pupil expenditure:	$2,600 OR ($2,600 – 450) = $2,150 (if recapture policy)
Total expenditure:	($2,600 × 1,500) = $3,900,000 OR ($2,150 × 1,500) = $3,225,000.

Note: Calculations assume no federal funding in total expenditure. Recapture policy occurs where states reduce district contribution by the amount in excess of the minimum foundation amount in an attempt to reduce inequity gaps between districts.

THE ROLE OF LOCAL GOVERNMENT

Local control of public education is essentially a phenomenon of the United States. The decentralized system was deemed to be an efficient way to ensure involvement of constituencies and to identify local needs. Making the local school district responsible for serving the diverse needs of the community is the reason that state governments use to justify the delegation of power and responsibility to local school boards in each district. However, it is that very decentralization that has perpetuated the inequities inherent in a system, because the value of property as a tax base varies between districts. It is the tax base that determines the taxing capacity and effort of each district; as the bases differ according to socioeconomic status, the abilities of local districts to generate equitable funding according to need fluctuate as well. Strayer and Haig's foundation program provided a practical design for equalizing local resources, but the foundation would have to be defined according to need rather than be limited by political and other constraints.

The degree of local fiscal control depends on the state-aid plan being used by state government. Burrup et al. (1996) point out that a big problem facing each state in providing equal educational opportunity for all is the extreme differences among districts' ability to pay for education as measured by the assessed valuation of taxable property per student to be educated. Perhaps the biggest issues facing local fiscal policymakers in obtaining adequate local funds are (1) the dependence on revenue from taxes on property, which is not a fair measure of the ability of people to pay, and (2) increasing competition for the local tax dollar. The inequities of the local property tax system are intensified by taxpayer disenchantment, such that tax hikes are not being tolerated and bond issues for schools are voted down (Association of Supervision 1999).

Source of Revenue for Local Funding

Despite its continued unpopularity and the obvious disparities between districts, real property tax remains the main source of revenue to local government for funding schools. In 1993, the Michigan legislature voted to eliminate the use of property taxes at the district level for funding schools and went with increased sales tax plus a statewide property tax to fill the void (Whitney 1994). This was an attempt to reduce the inequities caused by differences in local property wealth as mentioned earlier.

The revenue from property tax is determined by using the assessed value of real property as the base and applying a mill rate to it, such that the formula reads:

Equation 3.3
$$\text{yield} = \text{assessed value x mill rate}$$
where yield = the revenue generated
assessed value = market value of a proportional value of the real value
mill rate = a rate per $1,000 set by the state or local government
(It can be the assessed value of property divided by the net budget requirements in a given year.)

Twenty-five mills is interpreted as $25 per $1000 of assessed value, or .025 times the assessed value. This could also be written as 2.5 dollars per $100, or 25 cents per $10, or 2.5 cents per $1. Some states are using a "per $100-rate" instead of the old-fashioned mill rate.

Schools compete with all other services for these funds, and this competition adds to the inequitable distribution of funds; in poor districts with high-income maintenance needs, more funds tend to go towards support of families and to provide for health and unemployment services. Even at the very high millage or tax rate needed in poor districts to generate revenue, a lesser portion is available for schools than in wealthier districts. To compound the problem, the assessed property value is lower in poorer districts by definition, so even with high tax rates, the yield will be less. Further, property taxes allow for a tax break under federal personal tax rules; in high-income communities, there are greater opportunities to take advantage of this break than in low-income communities.

In applying the evaluation criteria mentioned earlier, it is clear that property taxes are regressive in nature and can create undue economic hardship, because the assessed valuation may not vary with the income flow from which the tax must be paid. However, the revenue from property taxes is reliable, and represents a large proportion of county or city funds, while the tax is easy to administer and difficult to avoid. Thus, property tax has remained a source of funds for public schools since the 1800s, despite several tax revolts and the growing resentment of the tax by an aging population with fewer children in school. The principal's job to convince the community of the value of education is a difficult one at this time.

THE ROLE OF THE FEDERAL GOVERNMENT

The Northwest Ordinance of 1787 showed federal government's recognition of the importance of education in developing the nation in terms of morality, economics, and equity. The ordinance marked the beginning of formal federal involvement by providing for the survey of land and the reservation of the sixteenth section of every township for building schools. Not all states received grants and not all states received the same amount of land. Utah, for example, was granted four sections in 1786, while the Oregon and other territories received two sections in 1848. Under the ordinance, states were expected to provide money for school purposes and were given some freedom in the use of granted lands in providing support for schools. In 1779, Congress submitted twelve amendments to the Constitution, later known as the Bill of Rights, one of which was to limit the role of the federal government in education—the Tenth Amendment. This forced the federal government to act through other authority or limited the federal government to indirect influence (Thompson et al. 1994). One such alternative authority was Article 1 of the Constitution concerning the need for a strong national defense, which Congress used to provide huge sums of money to education; another was the General Welfare Clause, also in Article 1. Under the General Welfare Clause, Congress was able to influence education through social and economic justice reform. Despite these efforts, the role of the federal government in education has been continually supportive but distant, except insofar as rulings in the U.S. Supreme Court have affected school finance policy. Nonetheless, the very presence of federal support lends credence to the importance of education in the society.

The federal government, through programs for education and related activities, has contributed vast sums of money to education overall, and to public elementary and secondary education in particular. In 1999, the federal government spent $12.8 billion dollars on public elementary and secondary education. The U.S. Department of Education provides most of these funds, which go to state education agencies where they are then allocated to local districts. Programs funded in this way include those for disadvantaged children, children with disabilities, programs for drug-free schools, mathematics and science programs, workforce development programs, and educational programs for migratory children. Department of Education funding provided directly to districts includes money for impact aid, bilingual education, and Indian education programs. Other federal agencies that spend substantial amounts on elementary and secondary education are the U.S. Department of Agriculture (through its child nutrition programs) and Health and Human Services (through its Head Start and other programs) (U.S. General Accounting Office 1998). For a detailed report on contributions by federal agencies on all federal programs geared towards education, see the Digest of Education Statistics put out each year by the U.S. Department of Education.

On-budget funding for federal programs is generally set through congressional appropriations. Almost 37 percent of the $34.5 billion spent by the federal government in fiscal year 1999 on elementary and secondary education came from the Department of Education, the largest provider of elementary and secondary funds. The department's major programs are Education for the Disadvantaged, Education for the Handicapped, school improvement programs (which include the Safe and Drug-free Schools programs, the Eisenhower Professional Development program, and the Innovative Education program), vocational and adult education programs, and Impact Aid (National Center for Education Statistics 2000). The federal government attempts to place funds where they can do the most good. This targeting reflects the historical development of the federal role in education as a kind of "emergency response system," a means of filling the gaps in state and local support for education when critical national needs arise (U.S. Department of Education 2000). One such need is clearly equity in education funding between districts and between states. In one GAO report, it was stated that in the 1991–1992 school year, federal funding was more targeted to poor students than state funds were in forty-five of the forty-seven states examined. On average, school districts received an additional $4.73 in federal funding per poor student for every $1 of funding received by each student, while state funding provided an additional $0.62. The amount of federal funding varied widely; at the high end, Alaska provided an additional $9.04 per student in federal funding and at the low end, West Virginia received only an additional $2.59 per student. See table 3.3 for a profile of North Carolina funding.

North Carolina also reported that the state targeted more funding of high-poverty districts in the school year 1996–1997, as did the federal government. In the 1996–1997 school year, federal funding for poor students increased due to changes in Title 1 legislation and regulations.

In addition, other federal education programs allocate funds on the basis of Title 1 funding formulas. For example, workforce development grants are partially based on these formulas; as a result, vocational education funding also increased in high-poverty districts. Federal government programs supporting children with disabilities, under the Individuals with

Table 3.3 Targeting to poor students (added amount allocated per poor student for every dollar allocated for each student), school year 1991–1992

State funding weight	$0.53
Federal funding weight	$4.97
Total funding weight (combined state and federal effect)	$1.05

Funding gap between districts with lowest and highest proportions of poor students

Local funds only	81%
State plus local funds	16%
Federal plus state plus local funds	7%

Source: US GAO, 1998

Disabilities Education Act, made changes in 1997 that are expected to result in targeting more funding to poor students. Funding patterns remained relatively unchanged in many other federal programs, such as Head Start, bilingual education, Indian education, and child nutrition programs, which cited no regulatory or legislative changes since 1991–1992 that would affect targeting to poor students.

The chart in table 3.4 highlights other noteworthy legislation enacted since the Northwest Ordinance.

Table 3.4   Selected federal programs for education

1917	Smith Hughes Act provided for grants to states for support of vocational education
1941	Amendment to Lanham Act of 1940 authorized federal aid for construction, maintenance, and operation of schools in federally impacted areas
1944	Servicemen's Readjustment Act—the GI Bill—provided assistance for the education of veterans
1946	National School Lunch Act authorized assistance through grant-in-aid and other means to states to assist in providing adequate foods and facilities for the establishment, maintenance, operation, and expansion of nonprofit school lunch programs
1950	Financial Assistance for Local Educational Agencies affected by federal agencies (Impact Aid)
1964	Civil Rights Act of 1964 authorized the commissioner of education to arrange for support of institutions of higher education and school districts to provide in-service programs for assisting instructional staff in dealing with problems caused by desegregation
1965	Elementary and Secondary Education Act of 1965 authorized grants for elementary and secondary school programs for children of low-income families; school library resources, textbooks, and other instructional materials for school children; supplementary educational centers and services; strengthening state education agencies and educational research and training
1981	Education Consolidation and Improvement Act of 1991 consolidated forty-two programs into seven programs to be funded under the elementary and secondary block grant authority
1994	Goals 2000: Educate America Act established a new federal partnership through a system of grants to states and local communities to reform the nation's education system
1995	Amendment to Elementary and Secondary Education Act of 1965 (U.S. Department of Education, 1997)
1997	Individuals with Disabilities Education Act Amendments 1997 (PL 105-17) amended IDEA to revise its provisions and extend through fiscal year 2002
1998	Workforce Investment Act of 1998 (PL 105-220) enacted the Adult Education and Family Literacy Act, and substantially revised and extended through fiscal year 2003 the Rehabilitation Act of 1973

Source: National Center for Education Statistics 2000

Source of Federal Funds

The major source of federal revenue is money from individual income taxes and, to a much lesser extent, corporate income taxes as shown in table 3.5 for fiscal year 1997. Funds for education are taken out of the physical, human, and community development section, but public education also benefits from funds given to individual federal agencies. Table 3.5 shows that income tax provides a stable source of funds. The income tax is considered to be a progressive tax because it has the ability to adjust with changes in the economic cycles and therefore varies with income. One of the key indicators of progressivity is that a party is no worse after the tax is applied; the relative wealth positions of different parties should not change. The personal income tax meets these conditions to a great extent. Though costly to administer, it is an easy tax to administer and compliance is almost guaranteed. As a revenue source, it is unquestionably satisfying. The report in the federal tax 1040 booklet each year provides updates on federal sources and uses of funds.

Mention has to be made that there is some attempt to ensure that taxes from different governmental agencies do not have a detrimental combined effect on the taxpayer. The Advisory Commission on Intergovernmental Relations (ACIR) is a federal commission created by the U.S. Congress in 1959 to monitor the operation of the federal system

Table 3.5 Federal government income and outlays, fiscal year 1999

Taxes	Income percent	Outlay	Percent of total
Personal income	48	Social Security, Medicare, and other retirement	35
Social Security, Medicare, unemployment, and other retirement	34	National defense, veterans, and foreign affairs	18
Corporate income	10	Social programs	17
Excise, customs, estate, gift, and miscellaneous	8	Net interest on debt	12
		Physical, human, and community development	9
		Law enforcement and general government	2

Source: Federal Income Tax 1040 booklet 2000

and to recommend improvements. The ACIR is a permanent, national bipartisan body composed of twenty-six members, who serve two-year terms and are representative of federal, state, and local governments and the public. As a continuing body, the commission approaches its work by addressing itself to specific issues and problems, the resolution of which would improve cooperation among the levels of government and the functioning of the federal system. One of the long-range efforts of the commission has been to seek ways to improve federal, state, and local government taxing practices and policies to achieve equitable allocation of resources, increased efficiency in collection and administration, and reduced compliance burdens upon the taxpayers. Many states have established their own ACIRs to study state and local developments within states (Shafritz 1992).

CONCLUSION

It is clear that funding for schools is increasingly dependent on intergovernmental revenue and resources, as well as on the policies implemented by the different levels. Of particular interest is the main source of revenue for government—taxes. The ACIR has taken on great importance in overseeing the burden of taxes placed by each agency at all levels of government if tax revolts are to be avoided. Although the structure of public school governance is such that the responsibility rests with local governments, funding through local property tax has not been successful in providing adequately or equitably for schools. Yet the limited role defined for the federal government leaves only the state governments to make the most effort to fund schools, and principals must use these funds wisely—not just to meet mandates, but to meet individual students' needs.

SUMMARY

- The role of the state in public education is delineated in the education clause of the state constitution; the state's responsibility is reflected in the proportion of total funds provided by the states to the public schools.

- The formulas used in calculating the amount of money appropriated in all the states and the District of Columbia are derived from eleven basic models. In all cases, the formulas are combined in one way or another and the aim is to achieve some level of equitable funding by trying to meet the needs of students. Emphasis is placed on local contribution rather than state contribution in the equalization formulas because it is important for principals to see their role in attaining equity and adequacy at the building level. Local property tax is discussed, as is the key role that this tax plays in funding schools.
- The role of the federal government is traced through the acts passed by Congress to provide federal funds to schools. The sources of tax revenues for federal government and the outlays for these funds show the greatest source is personal income taxes and the greatest outlay is to Social Security, Medicare, and other retirement benefits. Mention is made of the Advisory Commission on Intergovernmental Relations, whose duties include ensuring a reduced compliance burden on taxpayers.

DISCUSSION ITEMS

1. You are the principal in a middle school with a high proportion of special education students and you have to make a decision on an expenditure of $20,000 that has been given to the school as part of surplus funds from the state budget. What are the issues that need to be considered to ensure equity for special education students?

2. All principals have been asked by the state to evaluate the state's funding formula in terms of the impact on their school. Specifically, principals are asked to look at the state's precepts to see if they are being met at the building level at rural, small, urban, and high-poverty districts. Precept A) educational needs of at least 90 percent of the students should be met; Precept B) at least 90 percent of the students can read at grade level; and Precept C) at least 90 percent of the students must meet the eighth-grade standard established for the school exit exam in the twelfth grade.

3. The State Board of Education has created intervention teams to meet the particular needs in schools with low test scores. Your

school is one such and you need to justify the expenditure of funds for the team in order to help students. How would you do this?

4. You have been asked to justify the appropriation of Title 1 funds for your school. Further, if you do not get sufficient amounts, you can apply for other federal funds by justifying the need. What issues would you cite?

5. The federal and state governments have just published a request for proposals on providing schools with computers. Develop a financial proposal to submit to obtain funds for your school. Are there other sources from which you can seek funds should you not win these competitive funds?

6. Assume that you are representing teachers in a high-poverty school district with heavy local taxes and huge demand for noneducational services. What changes in general and or categorical aid you might suggest to help the school?

7. Define each of the following and explain their relevance to school finance: tax, tax burden, progressivity, ACIR, neutrality, ability to pay, benefit principle, assessed value, tax base, income tax, property tax, direct tax, millage.

8. The property tax is said to be regressive. Do you agree? Why or why not?

9. What are the features of the percentage-equalization plan and the foundation plan for state financial planning?

CHAPTER 4

Education and the American Judicial System

In order to understand the significance of court rulings in school finance cases, it is instructive to get some background on the American court system. The United States has a dual judicial system, state and federal. There are four types of state courts: general jurisdiction (called district or circuit courts), special jurisdiction, small claims courts, and appellate courts, sometimes called courts of appeals or supreme courts. Some states, such as New York and California, have intermediate appellate courts (Auerbach et al. 1961). The federal court system includes at least one district court in each state and usually more than two; eleven courts of appeals, one in each of the eleven federal judicial circuits; and courts established by Congress to handle special problems or to cover special jurisdictions The Supreme Court of the United States is the highest court in the land, beyond which there is no redress.

THE FEDERAL COURT ARENA

In the landmark case *Brown v. Board of Education* (374 U.S. 483, 1954) in Kansas, the inequality of educational opportunity under the law, the "separate but equal" provision in most states with segregated school systems, was overturned. The U.S. Supreme Court held that education is vital to the health and well-being of the nation and its citizens and that education is perhaps the most important function of state and local governments. Further, education is a right that must be made available to all on equal terms. Thus, the Court invoked the equal protection clause of the Fourteenth Amendment in terms of race as a suspect class and confirmed a fundamental right to education. Although this case was brought on the basis of racial equality, it had implications for school finance because an essential part of "separate" was inequitable and inadequate funding of some school districts by the state.

In *Burrus v. Wilkerson* (310 F.Supp.572, affirmed mem., 397 U.S. 44, 1969) in Virginia, and *McInnis v. Shapiro* (293 F.Supp 327 [N.D. III], 1968; 394 U.S. 322, 1969) and *McInnis v. Ogilvie* (394 U.S. 322, 1969) in Illinois, plaintiffs tried to use the conditions established in *Brown* to gain fiscal equality in educational opportunity. Federal courts essentially refused to intervene on the basis that the Fourteenth Amendment did not provide protection for unequal revenue; that school finance issues should be dealt with by the legislative branch according to the separation powers in the absence of clear invidious discrimination; and that there was a lack of judicially manageable standards. As Thompson et al. (1994) put it, the absence of equality was not the same as denial of equality. In *San Antonio Independent School District v. Rodriquez* (411 U.S. 1, 1973) in Texas, after the federal district court ruled the Texas school finance system unconstitutional under the Fourteenth Amendment, the U.S. Supreme Court on appeal ruled there was no distinct suspect class being discriminated against and that education was not seen as a fundamental right—thus remanding the case to the state and upholding legislative prerogative.

THE STATE COURT ARENA

Since the Rodriquez case, state courts have been the arenas for the search for equitable solutions to funding discrepancies between school districts, and to a much lesser extent, within school districts. At issue is not the deficiency in funding per se, but the qualitatively different levels of education available to students of different races, socioeconomic status, and communities. The intent of the court's decisions in the different states over time has only generated minimal changes in the qualitative difference. The most significant case is *Serrano v. Priest* (487 P.2d 1241, 1971), which had already been decided at the state supreme court in California before the Rodriquez decision. In *Serrano*, the court decided that the school finance plan violated federal and state constitutional guarantees of equal protection, that education could be seen as a fundamental right, and that a suspect class had to be defined according to school district wealth. Wise's (1969) argument on education as a fundamental right, and Coons et al.'s (1970) argument on fiscal neutrality, were validated in this case. The court not only applied what is known as the minimal scrutiny test but the strict judicial test as well, which were not applied in the federal court in school finance cases. The minimal scrutiny test simply queries the government's reason for interdistrict differences in funding, and the state must establish a rational relationship between the laws and the differences in funding. Under strict judicial scrutiny, the state has to show a compelling interest for its actions and that there is not a less discriminatory policy for its action (Sparkman 1990). This case became a catalyst for education finance reform across the nation as state courts became clogged with battles over inequities in school funding. Other cases of significance include *Robinson v. Cahill* (287 A.2d 187 [N.J. Super 1972], affirmed as mod., 303 A2d273, 1973) in New Jersey; *Board of Education, Levittown Union Free School District v. Nyquist* (408 N.Y.S.2d 606, 1978) in New York; *Hornbeck v. Somerset County Board of Education* (458 A.2dn758, 1983) in Maryland; *Rose v. Council for Better Education* (790 S.W.2d 185,1989) in Kentucky; and *Leandro v. State* (N.C. No. 179PA96, 1997) in North Carolina.

In *Robinson*, the case prevailed solely on the education clause of the state, thus allowing for careful analysis of state-aid formulas to see if equal protection laws of the state were upheld. The New Jersey legislature did not respond to court mandates; in July 1976, the New Jersey Supreme Court essentially closed down the entire school system by enjoining the expenditure of state funds for schools. The state legislature then designed a new school finance system and enacted a new tax system that allowed for local property tax relief (Odden and Picus 1992). In *Board of Education, Levittown Union Free School District v. Nyquist* (1978) in New York, *Hornbeck v. Somerset County Board of Education* (1983) in Maryland, and *Leandro v. State* (1997) in North Carolina, the issue of municipal overburden was raised. The plaintiffs claimed that inner-city school districts have huge demands for noneducational services such as welfare, underprepared students, health and welfare needs, and language difficulties; hence, the state minimum amount for basic education was not sufficient to provide for education and noneducation. For a state-aid formula to be adequate and equitable, additional funds should be provided for excessive education and non-education needs; otherwise, students are functionally excluded from the educational process.

The issue of adequacy was addressed in chapter 2, but it is worth mentioning here as the basis for *Rose v. Council for Better Education* (1989) in Kentucky and *Leandro v. State* (1997) in North Carolina. In New York, the court in *Campaign for Fiscal Equity et al. v. State of New York* (No. 111070/93, decided January 10, 2001) outlined elements of adequacy for students in the state. The entire education system was overturned in Kentucky as the state supreme court found that not only was the finance program inadequate and inequitable but the whole system was inequitable. The precedent currently being set in North Carolina is worth keeping a close eye on because the case is being tried in trial court in one of the low-wealth districts, in a lawsuit where witnesses will be called to testify about their educational experiences in the district. There is growing concern about the restrictive influence of property-rich districts in state legislatures and the impact this has on school finance issues.

In summary, as reported by Education Commission of the States (1998), the education finance system in eighteen states was deemed unconstitutional by the courts (table 4.1), and in another eighteen states, the system was upheld as constitutional (table 4.2). Although there were similarities in the facts of the lawsuits, there were differences in circumstances, current state policies, and other issues peculiar to the situation to allow for different ruling results, and hence the policy outcomes.

The National Center for Education Statistics report (cited in tables 4.1 and 4.2) has been used to address the continuing problems of inequalities in the fiscal capacities of school districts that result in unequal spending and educational opportunity due to heavy reliance on the tax bases of the school districts for funding (fiscal neutrality issue), inequalities in educational spending and opportunities, and inadequate educational opportunities. It should be noted that cases cited here stretch from 1971 through to 1997 and there are several cases currently in litigation dealing with these same issues. Since 1997, there have

Table 4.1   Education finance systems ruled unconstitutional

State	Decision date	Case
Alabama	1993 (lower court ruling served as final decision as case was not successfully appealed by state)	Opinion of the Justices, 624 So. 2d 103; Ex Parte (Ala 1993) Ex Parte James, 713 So. 2d 869 (Ala. 1997)
Arizona	1994	Roosevelt Elementary School District No. 66 v. Bishop, 179 Ariz. 233, 877 P 2d 806 (1994)
Arkansas	1983, 1994 (lower court ruling served as final decision as case was not successfully appealed by state)	Dupree v. Alma School District, 279 Ark. 340, 651 S.W. 2d 90 (1983) Tucker v. Lake View School District No. 25, 323 Ark. 693 917 S.W. 2d 530 (1996)
California	1971	Serrano v. Priest, 5 Cal 3d 584, 487 P. 2d 1241 (1971) (Serrano I)
Connecticut	1977	Horton v. Meskill, 172 Conn. 615, 276 A.2d 359 (1977)
Kentucky	1989	Rose v. Council for Better Education, 790 S.W. 2d 186 (Ky. 1989)
Massachusetts	1993	McDuffy v. Secretary of the Executive Office of Education, 415 Mass, 545, 615 N>E> 2d 516 (1993)
Missouri	1993 (lower court ruling served as final decision as case was not successfully appealed by state)	Committee for Educational Equality v. State of Missouri, 878 W.W. 2d 446 (Mo. 1994)
Montana	1989	Helena Elementary School District No. 1 v. State, 236 Mont. 44, 769 P.2d 684 (1989), amended, 784 P.2d 412 (1990)
New Hampshire	1997	Claremont School District v. Governor, 142 N.H. 462, 703 a.2D 1353 (N.H. 1997)
New Jersey	1973 and 1990	Robinson v. Cahill, 62 N.J. 473, 303 A.2d 273 (1973) Abbott v. Burke, 119 N.J. 287,575 A. 2d 359 (1990) (Abbott II)
Ohio	1997	DeRolph v. State, 78 Ohio St3d 193, 677 N.E.2d 733 (1997)
Tennessee	1993	Tennessee Small School Systems v. McWherter, 851 S.W. 2d 139 (Tenn. 1993)
Texas	1989	Edgewood Independent School District v. Kirby, 777 S.W.2d 391 (Tex. 1989)

Table 4.1 Continued.

State	Decision date	Case
Vermont	1997	Bringham v. State of Vermont, 166 Vt. 246, 692 A.2d 384 (1997)
Washington	1978	Seattle School District No. 1 v. State, 90 Wash, 2d 476, 585 P.2d 71 (1978)
West Virginia	1979	Pauley v. Kelly, 162 W.Va. 672, 255 S.E.2d 859 (1979)
Wyoming	1980 and 1995	Washakie County School District v. Herschler, 606 P.2d 310 (Wyo. 1980) Campbell County School District v. State, 907 P.2d 1238 (Wyo. 1995)

Source: Education Commission of the States 2000

Table 4.2 Education finance systems upheld as constitutional

State	Decision date	Case
Alaska	1997	Kaysayulie v. State, No. 3AN 97-3782 Civ. (Superior Court, filed 1997)
Arizona	1973	Shofstall v. Hollins, 110 Ariz. 88, 515 P.2d 590 (1973)
Colorado	1982	Lujan v. State Board of Education, 649 P.2d 1005 (Colo. 1982)
Georgia	1981	McDaniel v. Thomas, 248 Ga. 632, 285 S.E.2d 156 (1981)
Idaho	1975	Thompson v. Engelking, 96 Idaho 793, 537 P.2d 635 (1975)
Maryland	1983	Hornbeck v. Somerset County Bd. Of Educ. 295 Md. 597, 458 A.2d 758 (1983)
Michigan	1973	Milliken v. Green, 389 Mich. 1,203N.W2d 457 (1972), vacated, 390 Mich. 389, 212 N.W.2d 711 (1973)
Minnesota	1993	Skeen v. State, 505 N.W.2d 299 (Minn, 1993)
New York	1982	Board of Educ. Levittown Union Free School Dist. v. Nyquist, 57 N.Y.2d 127, 439 N.E.2d 359 (1982)
North Dakota	1994	Bismarck Public School District #1 v. State, 511 N.W.2d 247 (N.D. 1994)
Ohio	1979	Board of Education v. Walter, 58 Ohio St.2d 368, 390 N.E.2d 813 (1979)
Oklahoma	1987	Fair School Finance Council of Oklahoma, Inc. v. State, 46 P. 2d 1135 (Okla. 1987)

Table 4.2 Continued.

State	Decision date	Case
Oregon	1976 and 1991	*Olsen v. State*, 276 Ore. 9, 554 P.2d 139 (1976) *Coalition for Equitable School Funding, Inc. v. State*, 311 Or. 300, 811 P.2d 116 (1991)
Pennsylvania	1979	*Danson v. Casey*, 484 Pa. 415, 399 A.2d 360 (1979)
Rhode Island	1995	*City of Pawtucket v. Sundlun*, 662 A.2d 40 (R. I. 1995)
Virginia	1994	*Scott v. Commonwealth*, 443 S.E.2d 138 (Va. 1994)
Washington	1974	*Northshore School Dist. No. 417 v. Kinnear*, 84 Wash.2d 685, 530 P.2d 178 (1974)
Wisconsin	1989	*Kukor v. Grover*, 148 Wis. 2d 469, 436 N.W. 2d 569 (1989)

Source: Education Commission of the States 2000

been partial adjustments to state finance plans. In 1998, in New Mexico, for example, the state court ruled that the state's formula for distributing capital outlay funds was unconstitutional (http://www.edweeek.org). In 1999, the superior court in Alaska ruled the funding system unconstitutional in *Kasayulie v. State*; in Idaho in 1998, the state supreme court remanded the case *Idaho Schools Equal Educational Opportunity v. State* to the district court to determine whether the funding system was adequate; in 2001 in North Carolina, the superior court is finalizing its rulings on *Leandro v. State*; and in New York, on January 10, 2001, the state supreme court ordered the state legislature to draw up a new funding system by September 15, 2001 (Education Commission of the States 2000; http://www.cfequity.org/bottom.htm; Judge critical 2000).

Framework for Examining Equity

State legislatures, plaintiffs, and defendants in courts across the nation have relied on the measurement of equity to justify claims of race discrimination, wealth inequities, and more recently, inadequacy in school finance systems. A brief overview of the framework that has emerged as standards of measure, using students as the object for measurement and per pupil expenditure (PPE) as a variable, is outlined in table 4.3.

Table 4.3 Framework for measuring equity

Measure	Results and use	Equity measure
Mean: sum of all PPE in state divided by number of districts	average PPE in state; comparison between mean and actual PPE in any district to see deviations from mean	weak
Variance: average of the squared deviation from the mean PPE	the smaller the value of the calculation the less inequity; allows for testing for significance between groups as all observations are included	strong
Standard deviation: the square root of the variance	the smaller the value of the calculation the less inequity	strong
Co-efficient of variation: standard deviation divided by the mean	expressed as a ratio with a value between '0' and '1'; smaller value demonstrates less inequity	strong
Range: difference between highest and lowest PPE in school districts	the smaller the difference the lesser the inequity in the state	weak
Restricted range: difference between PPE at the 5th and 95th percentile	the smaller the difference the lesser the inequity in the state; reduces distortion in the measurement caused when using the two extremes	moderate
Federal range ratio: difference between PPE at the 5th and 95 percentile divided by the PPE at the 5th percentile	the smaller the resulting ratio the less the inequity; used originally by federal government to measure states' level of wealth neutrality as set by federal guidelines	moderate
McLoone Index: sum of PPE below the median divided by sum of required PPE if all districts below the median were at the median level; used to measure equity in the lower half of a distribution; designed specifically for school finance	ratio with a value between '0' and '1' where values closer to '1' means less inequity. It is possible for result to be greater than '1' if PPE of a group of districts is close to the median PPE value	strong
Gini coefficient: an economist's measure of income equality between percentages of the population	value between '0' and '1'; smaller value means lesser inequity	strong
Pearson correlation and regression: statistical measure of relationship between variables; for example, PPE and district wealth	correlation value ranging from '−1' to '+ 1'; a measure of fiscal neutrality; a value of '0' means no relationship, other values suggests some relationship; regression measures strength and cause of relationship	strong

CONCLUSION

Typically, inequities have been based on wide gaps in per pupil expenditures between districts, and on the fact that the differences can be traced to finance systems that rely on unequal tax bases as source of local funds. It has also become apparent over the years that filing suit using state-education clauses is different from using the equal protection strategy as a remedy. As states took note of the demands of plaintiffs in these cases, state-aid formulas were adjusted to reflect equalization measures (see chapter 3); however, little qualitative change has occurred. Demands in the courts have been more for "adequacy of funding"—terminology that in some instances remained dormant in state constitutions, especially in the differences evident in school facilities and outcomes, given the accountability models being used for evaluation in many states. At least forty states have had education finance litigation since the early seventies and many are still dealing with the initial issues raised in the first case in the state (Texas, California, and New Jersey, for example). However, the early cases forced state legislatures and state departments of education to move to increasingly fairer funding formulas for school districts; as more attention is paid to differences within districts, the equalization attempts could bear fruit at the level of local education agencies.

SUMMARY

- The impact of the courts is traced through the federal and state court systems, as the ruling in the first case examined, *Brown v. Board of Education* (1954), came from the U.S. Supreme Court. Four other cases were also taken to the federal court system; however, since the early seventies when the ruling in the Rodriquez case that education was the concern of state legislatures, school finance cases have been tried in the state courts.
- An overview of such litigation in all relevant states is provided. It is noted that the issues being litigated have not changed much since the earliest cases. This chapter also provides an introduction to some of the accepted statistical measures used by the courts to determine the level of inequity, if any.

DISCUSSION ITEMS

1. Your school district is one of the plaintiffs in an equity lawsuit against the state board of education. As principal of a school in one of the high-poverty districts, you have been asked to testify. What points would you make concerning the availability of resources for your students? Develop a comparative analysis with other schools within your district and schools in other districts in the state.
2. If you were asked which statistic best measures equity in your state, which would you choose? Why? Compare and contrast the accuracy and utility of the level of equity measured by each statistical method cited.
3. Describe the impact of the courts on school finance policy since the early 1970s through to the beginning of the twenty-first century.

CHAPTER 5

Budgeting and Cash
Management at the School Level

The school budget could be seen as a financial plan designed to enable the users to carry out policy for a fiscal year, and make plans for mid- and long-range periods. That is, the budget is a document that enables the principal to incorporate needs and information from below (teachers and staff in the school and community), as well as requirements and limitations from above (the district, county, state, and national levels of government). It is the planning document that will also be used at the end of a given period to evaluate performance of the immediate past period and used for changes and planning for the next period. The effectiveness of the budget depends on an understanding of, and commitment to, meeting goals as well as knowledge about sources and uses of funds so that the best possible implementation is possible to meet student needs. Furthermore, budgets provide historical data for evaluation of the extent to which educational policy and goals have been implemented or met.

This view of budget takes it out of the realm of just being a financial report to a document that holds the dreams and wishes and plans for a school that can enable the principal to run a successful learning organization. The budget is not a one-time plan; it is a dynamic document that requires continuous monitoring to maintain control and provide feedback for the flexibility necessary in a school. Bartizal (1942) suggested years ago that budgets be developed at the local school level—the point of contact with the students being served. Swanson and King (1997) maintain that school personnel cannot make meaningful curricular decisions without the authority to also make the necessary resource commitment decisions that enable the implementation of those curricular decisions; school-based decision making must include school-based budgeting as an integral component. This chapter provides an overview of budgeting, as well as sample forms that are usually required at the school level.

SCHOOL-LEVEL BUDGETING

One of the main functions of the principal is to manage revenues and expenditures so that educational goals are achieved in the most efficient way. Budgeting is the linchpin on which later phases of the accounting and evaluation process hang; it also provides the framework for nonmonetary resources and shows the implementation of education policies. Perhaps Herman and Herman (1997) described the budget best when they identified four basic functions of school site-based budgeting: 1) income and resources generation, 2) allocation concepts, 3) expenditure concepts, and 4) management concepts. These functions can be generalized to the budget process in schools without site-based management. Indeed, many schools currently provide a budget to the district superintendent, whose staff combines all budgets into the district's budget to be presented to the school board. Income and resource generation is generic to any budget-planning process. In states or districts with more centralized control, a good portion of revenue and resources will be provided by state funds and less from local funds. Federal funds vary according to the category of need into which the school falls, the size of the school's vocational education program, the school's proximity to a federal facility, and the proportion of students who fall under the Individuals with Disabilities Act, are considered members of migrant families, or qualify for Title 1 funds.

In addition, at the individual school level, revenue is generated from fund-raising activities, product sales of items made in the school, ticket sales from activities, donations from parent-teacher associations or other business and community organizations, interest earned on deposits or other investments, gains or losses on sales or investments, and various fees applied to particular services. Clearly, the sources of these funds will vary between levels of schools. For example, there may be more events where tickets are sold at the high school level than at the elementary level, but the accounting principles remain the same. It is these latter sources that are of interest here. The principal's responsibility at the individual school includes developing allocation strategies, deciding on expenditure patterns, and managing the portion of the budget dedicated to funds generated at the school.

BASIC ACCOUNTING PRINCIPLES

Accounting tasks traditionally were associated mainly with control in the past; today, they have been expanded to include the contemporary concept of accountability within the school, within the educational system, and outside of the school to taxpayers in the community (Hack et al. 1998). Because public schools are government organizations, they operate on a fund accounting system that is established to carry on specific activities or attain certain objectives of a school, according to special legislation, regulations, or other restrictions. In defining a fund, NCES (1990) stated that it is a fiscal entity with a self-balancing set of accounts recording cash and other financial resources. The fund classification adopted by NCES for schools includes the following:

Governmental Funds Types

General funds account for all financial resources of the school, except those required to be accounted for in another fund

Special revenue funds account for the proceeds of specific revenue sources (other than expendable trusts or major capital projects) that are legally restricted to expenditures for specified purposes (for example, federal grants-in-aid).

Capital projects funds account for financial resources used to acquire or construct major capital facilities (other than those of proprietary funds and trust funds). The most common source of revenue in this fund would be the sale of bonds.

Debt service funds account for the accumulation of resources for, and the payment of, general long-term debt, principal, and interest.

Proprietary Funds

Enterprise funds account for operations that are financed and operated in a manner similar to private business enterprises, where the stated intent is that the costs (expenses, including depreciation and indirect costs) of providing goods or services to the students or general public on a continuing basis are financed or recovered primarily through user charges (for example, food service programs).

Internal service funds are used for the operation of school functions that provide goods or services to other school functions, other schools, or other governmental units, on a cost-reimbursable basis (for example, central printing and duplicating).

Fiduciary Funds

Trust and agency funds account for assets held by a school in a trustee capacity or as an agent for individuals or private organizations, other governmental units, and/or other funds (for example, funds for parent-teacher organizations).

Much of the transaction of the liquid funds generated at the school level will be recorded on a cash basis rather than accrual basis. Cash basis can be defined as the basis of accounting where revenues are recorded only when actually received and only cash disbursements are recorded as expenditures (NCES 1990). Under accrual basis, revenues are recorded when earned or when levies are made, and expenditures are recorded as soon as they result in liabilities, regardless of when the revenue is actually received or the payment is actually made. It is usually required that funds (above some predetermined minimum) collected in a school be deposited in a designated bank with appropriate authorized signatures. No funds should be expended in cash before being deposited nor should personal checks be cashed from monies received. Deposits should be made in the time specified by the school district guidelines. Partly because of the time lag involved in government purchasing and contracts, principals have to be aware of encumbered funds. Encumbrances are commitments which are chargeable to a revenue account and for which part of the revenue is reserved. Encumbrances cease when paid or when actual liability is established. If accounts are kept on the accrual basis, then the amount reflects total charges incurred, whether paid or not, as current expense. For example, a principal orders materials for a fundraiser and the cost is $600, payable in sixty days. The cost of $600 has to be reflected in accounts payable account until the money is actually paid out to the vendor. So while the cash account would not show the reduction of $600 immediately, the principal has to be aware of the encumbered $600 when considering available funds. However, although the reporting steps differ, the principles of recording transactions are similar:

- report on cash basis available at beginning of fiscal year
- report on estimated cash to be generated during fiscal year
- report on estimated expenditures for fiscal year
- report on estimated balance of cash at end of fiscal year
- report on possible categories during fiscal year

The definition of terms such as "cash" and "expenditures" are rooted in allowable items under state law, as well as under general accounting principles. This highlights the differences and similarities between business and public school accounting. The school exists within the confines of fiscal controls placed on it by the state where revenues, for example, are limited to taxation, gifts, tuition, fines, fees, and transfer payments from state and federal governments (Hack et al. 1998). Because of the rules imposed by state and federal governments, schools use fund accounting with separate accounts for each fund. For schools, there is a further need to meet generally accepted definitions of the educational arena (Handbook from NCES; materials from Governmental Accounting Standards Board [GASB], Financial Accounting Standards Board [FASB], and American Institute of Certified Public Accountants [AICPA]). With the automation of the accounting process in most schools, the actual posting of transactions (that is, the bookkeeping) is done on computers; however, it is advantageous for principals to understand the input so as to effectively interpret the output. Furthermore, the principal needs to be familiar with the chart of accounts to verify that items are posted to the correct account. Bookkeeping is only one part of an accounting system that also involves recording, classifying, summarizing, reporting, and interpreting the results of the financial activities throughout the fiscal year (NCES 1990).

A brief explanation of FASB and GASB is necessary. FASB is a private sector organization that is an operating unit of the Financial Accounting Foundation. It sets standards for use in general purpose financial reporting according to the following principles and requirements: to govern the preparation of general purpose financial statements, to enhance the usefulness of financial statements by requiring the presentation of relevant information, and to create a reasonable degree of standardization among reporting entities, thus increasing the usefulness of financial statements and their credibility (FASB). GASB, also part of the Financial Accounting Foundation, was organized to establish standards of financial accounting and reporting for state and local government entities. The GASB function is important because external financial reporting can demonstrate financial accountability to the public and is the basis for investment, credit, and many legislative and regulatory decisions (Governmental Accounting Standards Board 2000).

FINANCIAL ACCOUNTING

Financial accounting is based on the principle that:

> Assets (items of value owned by the school) – Liabilities (debt the school owes) = Equity

In school accounting, however, the term equity is not used. Instead, the equation becomes:

> Assets – Liabilities = Fund Balance, or Assets = Liabilities + Fund Balance

This equation must be in equality (balanced). The rules for making an entry can be seen in a simple accounting format that allows for date of transaction and description of transaction.

Asset accounts are increased by debiting (debit side is left side), and liability and fund balance accounts are increased on the credit side (credit side is right side). Usually, a double-entry system is used. Double entry means that in each transaction, the amount of debit equals the amount of credit so that every action is self-balancing. The illustration in table 5.1 can serve to clarify the system.

The illustration is a summary view of the process. Initially, when a transaction takes place, it is recorded in a journal and then posted to an account that is established for each asset, each liability, and each fund

Table 5.1 Illustration of debits and credits

At the beginning of the fiscal year, July 1, the cash balance in the bank for ABC School is $15,000. The school is to receive an additional $20,000 from the county (that is, accounts receivable); and there is $10,000 invested in a Certificate of Deposit at a designated bank.

The school's current assets on July 1, 2001:

	Debit	Credit
Cash in bank	$15,000	
County funds receivable	20,000	
Investment in CD		$10,000
Total current assets		$45,000

Current assets refer to cash and other items that are easily converted to cash. In contrast, fixed assets refer to less-liquid items, such as equipment and buildings.

The school also owes $5000 to the state for income tax withholding, unemployment insurance in the amount of $4000, and $14,000 for supplies.

The liabilities are:

	Debit	Credit
State income tax withholding	$5,000	
Unemployment insurance		$4,000
Accounts payable for supplies		14,000
Total liabilities		$23,000

Hence, from the accounting equation Assets = Liabilities + Fund Balance:
  $45,000 = 23,000 − Fund Balance or $45,000 − 23,000 = Fund Balance
  $45,000 − 23,000 = $22,000

balance account. During the month, each transaction is entered first to a general journal (table 5.1), then to an individual account, and lastly to the general ledger, which is the place where all accounts come together. At the end of the month, each account is then balanced (that is, the difference between debits and credits is determined) and financial statements are derived from the information. If posting to the accounts has been done correctly, the total of all the debit balances should equal the total of all credit balances. To test this, a trial balance is prepared, where the trial balance is a listing of all the accounts and the amounts as they appear in the general ledger.

Once it is determined that the trial balance is correct, the other financial statements (such as the balance sheet, revenue, appropriations and expenditures, and cash flow reports) can be developed. The cash flow statement would be of particular interest to principals, since the accounts generated at the school level are usually based on cash activities. Samples of a district-level combined balance sheet, combined statement of revenues, expenditures, and changes in fund balance statements are provided in appendix C.

Table 5.2 Illustration of trial balance sheet

ABC Elementary School
General Fund
General Journal

Date	Account Title	Post Acct.	Debit $	Credit $
7/1/01	Cash in bank	100	5,000	
	Certificate of deposit	211	5,000	
	Contracts payable	420		5,000
	Fund balance	600		5,000
	To record beginning balances			
7/2/01	County taxes receivable	520	20,000	
	Revenue from local taxes	500		20,000
	To record funds from local taxes			
7/3/01	Expenditure on instructional supplies	510	4,000	
	Accounts payable	400		4,000
	To record purchase of supplies			
7/4/01	Cash in bank	100	100,000	
	Revenue state sales tax	300		100,000
	To record funds from state			
7/5/01	Salaries for temporary staff	530	30,000	
	Cash in bank	100		30,000
	To record payment to staff			
7/6/01	Accounts payable	400	2,000	
	Cash in bank	100		2,000
	To record payment on account			
7/7/01	Cash in bank	100	15,000	
	Taxes receivable	520		15,000
	To record receipt of funds			
7/8/01	Contracts payable	420	5,000	
	Cash in bank	100		5,000
	To pay on contracts payable			

ABC Elementary School
General Fund
General Ledger

Cash in Bank Account #100

Date	PR	Amount $	Date	PR	Amount $
7/1/01	2	5,000	7/5/01	2	30,000
7/4/01	2	100,000	7/6/01	2	2,000
7/7/01	2	15,000	7/8/01	2	5,000

Certificate of Deposit - Investment Account #211

Date	PR	Amount $	Date	PR	Amount $
7/1/01	2	5,000			

Accounts Payable Account #410

Date	PR	Amount $	Date	PR	Amount $
7/6/01	2	2,000	7/3/01	2	15,000

Contracts Payable Account #420

Date	PR	Amount $	Date	PR	Amount $
7/8/01	2	5,000	7/1/01	2	5,000

County Taxes Receivable Account #520

Date	PR	Amount $	Date	PR	Amount $
7/2/01	2	20,000	7/7/01	2	15,000

Fund Balance Account #600

Date	PR	Amount $	Date	PR	Amount $
			7/1/01	2	5,000

Revenue - County Taxes Account #500

Date	PR	Amount $	Date	PR	Amount $
			7/2/01	2	20,000

Revenue - State Taxes Account #300

Date	PR	Amount $	Date	PR	Amount $
			7/4/01	2	100,000

Expenditure - Instructional Supplies Account #510

Date	PR	Amount $	Date	PR	Amount $
7/3/01	2	4,000			

Salaries - Temporary Staff Account #530

Date	PR	Amount $	Date	PR	Amount $
7/5/01	2	30,000			

ABC Elementary School
Trial Balance
July 31, 2001

	Debit $	Credit $
Cash	83,000	
Certificate of deposit	5,000	
County taxes receivable	5,000	
Fund balance		5,000
Accounts payable		2,000
Revenue from county taxes		20,000
Instructional supplies	4,000	
Revenue from state		100,000
Salaries	30,000	
Total	$127,000	$127,000

Notes: The general ledger account page number is placed in the post column of the general journal after entry into the general ledger. The PR column in the general ledger is used to record the page of the general journal on which the entry is first made.

Debit entries in the general journal are made first while credit entries are indented after the debit entry to ensure the double entry system is maintained.

A balanced trial balance does not necessarily mean the entries are correctly placed in the proper accounts; it is therefore necessary to verify general ledger accounts even after trial balance is completed.

The principal will not have to develop these accounts, however, as much of the work on the budget and in the whole accounting process at the school level will involve completing federal, state, and district-level generated forms. These forms are used to document personnel time on task, which can be translated into data for payroll and time on task analysis. These forms are the equivalent to account notes attached to more sophisticated and detailed accounts. Also included is a sample of an individual school budget-planning document and school budget report in appendix C. Each state establishes a chart of accounts, which is a numbering system that allows for identification of the fund type, the school, and the category to which the money is applied and ensures that these categories are consistent from school to school. The number coded to each account helps with budgeting, planning, auditing, and evaluating, and when this information is combined with sophisticated technological systems, it is possible to identify the expenditure funds to the micro level—

the student. Of particular significance to the principal is the interpretation of the monthly school budget report, which shows the percentage of budget used, the budgeted amount for each line item, year-to-date expenditures, encumbrances, and the budget balance at the end of the period. Budget encumbrances occur when obligations are chargeable to an account and some of the appropriations are on hold. When the transactions are completed, the encumbrance ceases. The example of the budget-planning document in appendix C provides a picture of the necessary detail. The completion of the document should be done with careful thought.

BUDGET ADMINISTRATION

A key issue in budget administration is that of interpreting financial reports because it is in the analysis of these reports that the principal obtains information for planning. State laws usually cover such issues as investment of idle cash, selection of official depositary, frequency of deposit or investment, and the handling of funds generated at school level. However, it is the principal or fiscal manager at the school site who must interpret reports as well as generate the explicit reports that become the basis for financial and performance audits of the school's financial operations. As is stated in a special note to principals in the *Procedures Manual of Cumberland County, N.C.* (1994):

> It is essential for you to follow the law and accepted practices. The principal is held accountable for expenditure of funds allocated to the school. It is the principal's responsibility to establish sound bookkeeping and business practices for all receipts and expenditures regardless of the source of funds. This includes proper accounting of funds by organizations sponsored by the school. . . . The principal must assume the responsibility for financial planning as well as protecting school funds. . . . Make certain you are knowledgeable about the laws regarding the handling of school funds.

BUDGETING FOR TECHNOLOGY

What exactly comprises "technology" for school is a little unclear. In most instances, the term brings to mind pictures of computers on desks as well as ways of accessing the Internet. Although these are major components of the technology arena, the full gamut of resources includes CD-ROMs, videodisk players, and the latest disks and software to support the curriculum in each discipline at all levels. In 1995, it was estimated that by the year 2000, initial costs to set up a twenty-five-station computer laboratory would range from $11 billion per year for each school to $47 billion per year for a network in each classroom. At the high end, this amount would represent 3.9 percent of a school budget from kindergarten to twelfth grade (McKinsey 1995). To date, much of the funding needed to implement or enhance technology access in public schools has come from categorical monies provided by federal, state, and local governments and some private sources. This method of funding is usually characterized by restrictions and has little provision (if any) for maintenance costs or upgrades. Additional funds have to be sought to maintain a designated level of competence or to effect repairs. Furthermore, the acquisition of computers must be coupled with funding to provide infrastructure, train teachers and media personnel, and provide supporting materials such as workbooks. Infrastructure is becoming less important with the spread of wireless technology, which should reduce the cost of implementation and make assimilation into the current expenditure easier. In fact, many of the budget items for technology are new or relatively new to the budget line. Principals are usually limited to budgeting for line items established at the district level, whereas technology needs can be quite different from school to school.

Another issue is the fact that most educational expenditures occur annually and are tied to instructional programs that do not change dramatically from year to year. Establishing a technology budget is different in that the amount may change dramatically every two to three years, for example, if the school is to remain connected to the Internet, when manufacturers increase the speed of transmission so that faster modems are needed, which starts a chain reaction in software, memory, and interface equipment needs. It might be much more economical to lease computers and the concomitant pieces of the support system that lend themselves to leasing, rather than purchasing outright. Introducing technology into schools also changes the personnel needs, so this has to be taken into consideration when drawing up the personnel budget.

FINANCIAL REPORTING

Reporting is a major part of the accounting cycle because it is in the reporting that various interested parties (the county, state, and federal governments, the community, students, principals, and educational planners) are provided with a snapshot of operations. The principal should develop skills in interpreting financial reports in order to make meaningful decisions. School systems tend to use the format of the comprehensive annual financial report (AFR), which allows for comparison between schools, districts, and states, while forming a basis for accountability. The financial reports necessary in a school are of two main types: internal and external. Internal reports include comparison of budgeted versus actual revenues and expenditures; cash flow projections; building operations and maintenance costs; and the expenditure accounts. External reports include general financial/statistical summaries for use by legislators; specific reports of certain revenues and expenditures by program, for use by funding source(s); and program costs reports. Materials for these reports are collected from individual schools and the reports submitted from the principals. Financial reporting is sometimes only as good as the information provided through the accounting process, so the classification of funds and accounts in the uniform chart of accounts before the process begins is designed to make reporting information easier.

Principals are usually provided with specific guidelines and forms that standardize the data reported and provide the central office with checks and balances to help in developing financial reports. Each school is responsible for submitting an individual school budget, which is the collective work of various committees and parties associated with the school. Although the principal may not be directly involved in day-to-day financial activities, he or she is responsible for such activities in the school and should have a working knowledge of the required procedures. Principals are also responsible for ensuring successful audits of the school. The reports that are particularly useful to administrators at the district level are delineated by Hartman (1988) as:

- balance sheet listing all funds, which can be compared to the previous year's entries
- statements of revenue, expenditure, and changes in fund balances for all government funds

- statements of revenue, expenditure, and changes in fund balances (budgeted and actual) for general and special funds
- statements of revenue, expenditure, and changes in retained earnings (equity) for all proprietary funds, and
- statement of changes in financial position for all proprietary fund types

AUDITING

The audit is another tool to enable the principal to operate effectively. Candoli, Hack, and Ray (1992) define auditing as the study of accounting systems generally, and of specific accounts in particular, in order to ensure the accuracy and completeness of the accounting records of the districts. Audits serve several purposes: they help to find errors that occurred during the accounting procedure, they help to find ways to improve or enhance the accounting process, and they provide a means of showing how fiscal management is being used to meet the educational mission and goals. The audit can be a means of protecting the administrator (Thompson, Wood, and Honeyman 1994).

The single audit process is a series of audits used to provide a complete process of evaluation. Furthermore, audits can be financial or geared to monitor performance, internal, external, specific to a particular function, or general in nature. The process actually begins in the design and format of the accounting system that facilitates gathering of data conducive to activities involved in auditing. These activities include preparation of materials or pre-audit steps, the audit itself, and the post-audit steps. An audit can also be continuous if activities are built into the accounting process to facilitate continuous evaluation. This method is particularly easy if the accounting system is fully automated.

Preparing for an Audit

In order to prepare for an audit, the principal should ensure a minimum of the following steps are carried out:

- strengthen internal accounting procedures
- allow ample time to prepare for the audit

- prepare for the audit by collecting all relevant documents to support accounting records
- prepare all personnel for the process that will involve many of the school's staff

These steps are required for all types of audits. In the case of continuous internal audits, there are constant checks and balances to ensure that the accounting system can support a comprehensive audit by state, county, and/or federal government.

External audits are a formal examination of the financial records of a school by qualified outside personnel to verify the accuracy of those records and compliance with all statutory provisions. These audits are carried out by reputable independent auditing organizations, thus ensuring professional competence and objectivity. The accounting process is designed to provide financial reports that can assist in the audit function and provide response to audit findings (Thompson et al. 1994). The audits must meet the standards set by the American AICPA.

The performance audit is an objective and systematic examination of evidence for the purpose of providing an independent assessment of the performance of a governmental organization, program, activity, or function in order to provide information to improve public accountability and facilitate decision making by parties with the responsibility to oversee or initiate corrective action (N.C. state auditor, www. osa.state.nc.us/OAS/yellow/ybchap2.htm). Performance audits include economy and efficiency audits, as well as program audits. Economy and efficiency audits include determining whether the entity is acquiring, protecting, and using its resources (such as personnel, property, and space) economically and efficiently, the causes of inefficiencies or uneconomical practices, and whether the entity has complied with laws and regulations on matters of economy and efficiency. Program audits include determining the extent to which the desired results or benefits established by the legislature or other authorizing body are being achieved; the effectiveness of organizations, programs, activities, or functions; whether the entity has complied with significant laws and regulations applicable to the program; and whether the resources are being used to satisfy equity principles—especially vertical equity, which is paramount in school-level analysis.

Table 5.3 Student activity funds self-assessment checklist

Receipts

- prenumbered documents and tickets are used for all receipts
- all receipts are account verified
- receipts/cash registers indicate source of funds and cash versus checks
- receipts are deposited intact on a frequent basis
- all transfers of funds are documented

Expenditures

- have a proper accounting approval
- are for student purposes
- district purchasing policies are followed
- impress and petty cash claims are promptly processed
- credit memos are promptly processed
- invoices are matched to purchase orders and receiving documents before processing

Student activity funds represent a very small portion of total district funds, but are an integral part of school-level planning and budgeting. Taking control of these funds is crucial to a school principal and the school's bookkeeper or treasurer. The checklist provided by Cuzetto (1995) in table 5.3 is a good way to have constant oversight.

CONCLUSION

The principal is the administrator for the school budget, and is responsible for construction of the school's budget in a format acceptable for approval at the district, county, or state level, where approval means the budget has met statutory provisions. The role of the school business administrator becomes more important as education reform movements support increased local control, such as site- or school-based management systems. Researchers have reported findings from their research that show academic achievement is directly related to the quality of the school building, level of staff, and the quality of service provided by the principal or site manager. Under site-based management, the principal has to take on responsibilities previously carried out by others, perhaps at the central office. Technology has simplified these tasks to some degree but has not eliminated the need for the conceptual knowledge needed to make sound decisions.

The school administrator should have planning expertise to deal with organizational changes that result from new laws and regulations, new demographic patterns, changing educational needs, and changes in local conditions. The school administrator should also have financial expertise because no plan is complete without the funds to implement it. Furthermore, the personnel function becomes more important because education is labor intensive, with approximately 85 percent of the education budget allocated to salary and wage-related costs. Human skills, defined by Candoli, Hack, and Ray (1992) as the capacity to react to and interact with diverse clients, are also crucial. Yet it is important to realize that a school should not be expected to operate with the ethics and profit motive of a private business; rather, schools need to observe a standard of conduct that reflects generally accepted business procedures and practices while recognizing that the "service role" is the primary mission. A point that cannot be overemphasized is that school business administrators have a dynamic responsibility to respond to many, and often conflicting, forces.

If there is constancy, then it is in change—change in the political environment, in the framework in which decisions are made, and in the organizations in the communities around the schools. The availability of funding for resources is an area that is highly volatile and requires close control under site-based management if the state plays a lesser role in the school. The principal's role as political mediator in the local community becomes apparent when considering obtaining increased funds through local taxes (Kimbrough and Nunnery 1988). Management and leadership skills are also crucial in defining and resolving problems equitably. Budgeting for technology brings an added dimension to the process because of the short life span of computers and equipment needs. This is an additional area of challenge for principals who are themselves entering a fairly recently charted area.

Perhaps the initial step for the school business administrator is to answer the questions posed by Hack, Candoli, and Ray (1998): What are the educational needs that have business implications? What are the nature and the cost of each feasible alternative to meet a given educational need? What are the most efficient and cost-effective means to meet the educational needs as determined?

SUMMARY

- The budget is an enabling document for principals to achieve policy goals at the school level. The principal has to manage revenues and expenditures efficiently and must therefore develop budgeting skills to provide the framework for the nonmonetary accounting and evaluation processes. Of particular significance for principals are funds that are generated through school activities.
- Basic accounting principles are presented, and funds commonly found on school budgets are defined under three headings: governmental, proprietary, and fiduciary. Sources of materials useful to principals, such as the Governmental Accounting Standards Board, the Financial Accounting Standards Board, the American Institute of Certified Public Accountants, and a handbook provided by the National Center for Education Statistics, are presented. Illustrations of basic debit and credit entry practices are provided, as are examples of entries from general ledger through trial balance reporting.
- The chapter also provides material on budget administration and preparing for an audit. Budgeting for technology is alluded to, with emphasis on the need for the constant update of hardware and software.
- The budget is a dynamic document that must recognize change in political climate as well as in the organization and the school itself.

DISCUSSION ITEMS

1. You are the principal of a high school and it is football season. The bookkeeper is responsible for collection of money at the gate and refreshment stands. What instructions would you give the bookkeeper to ensure all policies and regulations are met?
2. Obtain a general fund statement from your school district and provide an explanation to the audience in a town hall meeting, where the community involvement strategies require monthly briefings and the audience has questioned the discrepancies between budgeted amounts and actual expenditure on key items, such as technology and special education.
3. Donning your hat as school manager, outline the steps needed for a successful audit to your teachers and staff.

CHAPTER 6

Financing School Facilities

During the period from World War II to the end of the 1960s, an unprecedented number of new schools were built. The rapid increase in student population, combined with migrations from rural areas to city and suburb, made necessary the construction of thousands of new schools. The decreasing rate of student growth in the 1970s and the later combining of schools caused a relaxation in the pressure for new construction. Migration to the cities continued, however, so the demand for construction in urban areas coincided with the decline in the tax capacities to fund schools. Construction of new schools was not considered a priority in urban areas. However, given the effect of the baby boom echo population wave (that is, given the rising number of annual births since 1977) and the burgeoning education lawsuits in several states, the adequacy of school facilities, which had taken second place to equity issues in much of the literature, is today in the forefront. Yet in the midst of the depreciation of some school facilities, there are model schools across the country that have contributed to the controversy about inequities in school funding because these schools are found in wealthy school districts right next to dilapidated schools in poorer districts in the same state. Such model schools are modern, well-designed institutions of learning with contemporary technology in all laboratories and libraries/media centers, as well as full-service physical and health education resources. (US GAO 1996).

The courts have alluded to the inadequacy of school facilities in several cases. In *Campaign for Fiscal Equity et al. v. State of New York* (No. 111070/93, decided January 10, 2001), in *Kasayulie v. State* (Alaska

1999), and in *Leandro v. State* (North Carolina No. 179PA96, 1997), the need for a public education adequate to the needs of all the children in each state was recognized. In *City of Cincinnati v. Walter* (Ohio 1976), reference was made to the facts that physical plants in a school district were substantially significant and obsolete, and that poorly lighted and inadequately maintained school buildings impair teaching and learning efficiency and have a negative effect on student morale and motivation. The state supreme court of Arizona observed that the quality of facilities is directly proportional to the value of a district's real property. The court noted disparities in the condition and age of buildings and the quality of classrooms and instructional equipment; some districts have schools that are unsafe, unhealthy, and in violation of building fire and safety codes (*Roosevelt Elementary School v. Bishop* [Arizona 877P.2d 806, 1994]). In *Pauley v. Kelly* (West Virginia 255 E2d 859, 1979), *Pauley v. Bailey* (324SE2d 128, 1984), *Helena Elementary School District v. State* (Montana 769 P.2d 684, 1989), and *Lujan v. Colorado State Board of Education* (Colorado 649 P.2d 1005, 1982), references were made to school facilities being part of the equation when studying inequitable issues in school finance.

The condition of school buildings across the nation has drawn national attention because the age of these buildings makes it impossible to ignore and the inequities observed in facilities in districts of differing wealth become glaringly apparent. Expenditure for capital outlay constitutes the largest difference in the spending patterns of low-wealth compared to high-wealth school districts. Overall spending for capital outlay in wealthy districts (poverty rate below 5 percent) is 76 percent higher than in poor districts (poverty rate over 25 percent). Schools in low-wealth districts have less to spend; hence, they sacrifice capital outlay expenditures first (Parrish and Fowler 1995). A report from the General Accounting Office (1996) stated that 60 percent of schools have at least one major building feature in disrepair, such as leaky roofs and crumbling walls, and over 50 percent have at least one environmental problem, such as poor indoor air quality. Because of the perception that federal programs—as well as state and local financing mechanisms—did not address facility needs of many of America's schools, Congress passed the Education Infrastructure Act of 1994 and appropriated $100 million for grants to schools for repair, renovation, alteration, or construction. These funds were eliminated in 1995 by legislative efforts to balance the budget. Therefore, there were no monies from the federal government for school facilities except through federal Impact Aid and special grants. In 1996, President Clinton launched the school construction initiative to help local communities and states rebuild the nation's schools. The initiative was spearheaded on the belief that schools did not have the physical infrastructure to allow students to meet the challenges of the twenty-first century. Many schools did not have the physical infrastructure to make the best use of computers, printers, and other equipment. Forty-six percent of schools reported inadequate electrical wiring for computers and communications technology, as well as insufficient technology elements (such as fiber optics cabling, phone lines for modems, and wiring for computers). Many school districts face the need to build new schools to accommodate enrollment growth. Public school enrollment in grades K–12 is expected to rise 20 percent between 1990 and 2004 (http://gopher.ed.gov/updates/con-sum.html).

Key elements of President Clinton's New School Construction Initiative were to provide up to 50 percent interest subsidy for new school construction and renovation. The initiative was intended to reduce interest costs on new school construction and renovation projects by up to 50 percent, with a sliding subsidy scale, depending on need. The interest reduction was equivalent to subsidizing $1 out of every $4 in construction and renovation spending. One of the key criteria in distributing funds to projects was to be the extent to which the spending is incremental—above what would have occurred without this initiative (Kickbush 1996).

METHODS OF FUNDING SCHOOL FACILITIES

Capital outlay expenditures in the context of public schools can be defined as expenditures for fixed assets, such as land, buildings, improvement and additions to buildings, and equipment, as well as the cost of maintaining and repairing equipment and buildings. These expenditures are presumed to have benefits for more than a year (at least three years) and usually involve commitment to large sums of money.

As Garms and others put it, funds for the purpose of building schools or facilities are classified as capital expense, and capital expenses are usually limited to the purchase of items of a permanent nature, normally divided into categories of land and improvements to land, buildings, and equipment (Garms et al. 1978). An important characteristic of capital expense is the unevenness of expenditure. Construction of a school in the first year may cost several million dollars, with expenditure in succeeding years being almost zero. This unevenness has important implications. Because construction of a new school is such a huge investment and since it is usually under the contract of local government, then financing it out of current revenues would mean large fluctuations in local tax rates to generate sufficient income each period.

The cost of building and maintaining school facilities has fallen mainly on local school districts, and the quality of these facilities has therefore been a function of local fiscal capacity. State constitutions have historically provided the funds derived from federal land grants that must be used exclusively for the current support of the common schools. Also, school buildings are seen as local community assets, enhancing property valuations, and therefore should be financed from local property taxes. During the early development of state-aid programs throughout the United States, it was generally assumed that provision by the state for current expense needs would release sufficient local funds for capital-outlay purposes. Since this did not prove to be the case, the popular method of funding construction is through borrowing. The methods identified in the literature are:

Current Revenues

Where local districts are fully or partially responsible for funding facility needs, financing through annual revenues from taxes levied in the current year is one option used. This method avoids interest costs because funds are made available before actual spending takes place. However, differences in the wealth and the tax base of school districts make this an inequitable method and make it unlikely that some districts will ever be able to afford to build or even maintain the condition of their buildings.

Sinking Funds

Sinking funds (also called building reserve funds) are essentially savings accounts of some kind where money accumulates with earned interest until it reaches some required level. While this method has its merits in that it facilitates long-range planning, the money earns interest, and the district is not incurring interest on its debt, it has the serious drawback of being subject to inflationary pressure on two sides. The value of the money falls if the inflation rate is higher than the interest rate being earned, and inflationary pressure on the cost of the building or repairs can make it difficult to achieve the required level of funds in the future.

Bonded Indebtedness

Bonded indebtedness occurs where the local district is allowed to issue general obligation bonds to borrow funds and commit them to school facilities. Bonds are simply IOUs that obligate the issuing agency to repay a loan, the principal amount, at a specified time, and the interest on the loan over a period of time. The person purchasing the bond or holding the IOU can choose to receive periodic interest payments, maybe quarterly, for a specified time until the principal is due. These bonds are usually called municipal bonds and have proven to be attractive because of their tax-exempt status. The bond process is usually protected by statutory regulations and limitations that vary from state to state. This method usually requires the involvement of the community, so a bond referendum is held whereby voters can make their wishes known. This is a complex procedure that is closely overseen by state agencies and involves oversight by professionals in the legal and financial fields. The role of the school principal in this process is key because he or she has to take leadership in building trust and community involvement.

States have tried to fulfill their obligations to school districts by applying the same funding mechanisms mentioned in chapter 3. Full state funding, equalization grants, percentage-matching grants, and flat grants have proven even less successful in providing for adequate facilities than for

equalization of school funding. State assistance loans that are used to provide direct assistance to local school districts create debt without the com-
plications of bonded indebtedness, but unless consideration is given to the
capacity of the district to repay the loan, the debt can add to inequity. In
addition, low-wealth districts, where the need may be greatest, would not
necessarily qualify for loans. States have also established state or local
building authorities as public corporations for the purposes of circum-
venting the restrictive taxing or debt limitations of local governments for
facilitating the construction of essential local school facilities (Swanson
and King 1997; Thompson et al. 1994). As separate public corporations
that do not operate schools, these agencies are not as restricted in their
borrowing ability; to some extent, they can operate to achieve some level
of fiscal equality for less-able districts in the arena of borrowing.

CHARTER SCHOOLS

The advent of charter schools adds a new dimension to any discussion on school facilities; in many states, these schools do not generally have access to the most common source of facility funding for
public schools: the ability to raise taxes or issue tax-exempt bonds.
Even if they are part of a local school district, they may not share in
the local or state construction funds because of competition or opposition from the more traditional schools. In a recent report, the
United States General Accounting Office reported that the sources of
funding available to charter schools include: (1) per pupil allocation
that a state or school district provides for operating public schools;
however, these schools may receive less than the average allocation
for the schools in the district; (2) loans which are not easily accessible; most charter schools are considered credit risks because they often have poor cash flow, lack a long credit history, have short-term
charters, or are administered by management teams with limited
business skills; and (3) donations of facilities, which rarely occurs.
A broader federal role in funding facilities in charter schools through
grants, direct loans, loan guarantees, loan pools, tax-exempt bonds,
and tax credits would provide some security for these schools (General Accounting Office 2000).

ROLE OF THE PRINCIPAL

The principal's role involves both the maintenance of plant and operations and the development of plans for new school buildings. The maintenance function can be seen as keeping buildings, equipment, and grounds in near-new condition through repair and replacement of parts (Thompson et al. 1994). This requires regular, skilled evaluation of the entire interior and exterior areas of the site, and of equipment for instructional and noninstructional purposes. The goal is to stay ahead of problems and effect repairs and changes in a timely manner in order to maintain the integrity of the facilities and equipment.

In the case of planning for a new school or a new building on a site, certain steps have been identified as minimally necessary.

Step 1:

Determine the extent of the need. This is done by developing projections of student enrollment for the district or school for the next five to ten years. Projections of enrollment can been done by using the cohort survival method or regression time-prediction method. The cohort survival method is based on enrollment by grade level, which is combined with the census estimates of preschool children in the district, examination of records of the number of live births, and adjustments for new entering students at each grade level. The regression line method assumes that at each grade level (or group of grades), the change in enrollments from year to year consists of a constant trend with random variations superimposed on it; that is, develop a line of best fit. Combining projections with data on student home location, and with analyses of present building capacity, can provide a picture of future needs.

Step 2:

Determine where construction will take place. If a new building is needed, then land has to be purchased, or the selection of an owned site in relation to the location of current and potential students is needed. Consideration could also be given to simple expansion of current buildings.

Step 3:

Work with an architect, and provide the architect with educational specifications, such as number of students to be housed and the kind of educational programs to be offered. Principals need to follow construction closely.

Step 4:

Sign off on completed building.

Step 5:

Select suitable equipment to be purchased.

IMPORTANCE OF SCHOOL FACILITIES

It is clear that students need schools and facilities, but the importance of quality is not clear. The guidelines for designing school buildings are usually provided by the state, and these guidelines differ from state to state. However, there are studies showing some relationship between provision of facilities and educational achievement or improvement. It can be argued that newer buildings and facilities are necessary to operate the more modern instructional programs, such as contemporary technology laboratories, classrooms, science laboratories, media centers, and vocational education centers. New types of buildings are needed to accommodate exceptional students and workers. To date, many buildings have been modified according to legal specifications, but newer buildings are allowing for more creativity in serving all populations. The fact that no close connection between facilities and educational achievement has been demonstrated does not mean that such a connection does not exist.

The size of a school is another important issue in terms of economies of scale, which dictate a minimum size. There are diseconomies of scale that are incurred in small schools, while very large schools obtain financial economies bought at the expense of student and teacher satisfaction. A smaller school usually develops a sense of community that is

not evident in a large school. Furthermore, in large schools, it is difficult for principals to interact with students and get to know them well.
Earthman et al. (1995) found in a study of North Dakota high schools,
a state with a relatively homogenous, rural population, a positive relationship between school condition and both student achievement and
student behavior. McGuffey (1982) reported that heating and air condi-
tioning systems appeared to be very important, along with special instructional facilities and the color of interior painting, in contributing to
student achievement. Proper building maintenance was also found to
be related to better attitudes and fewer disciplinary problems. Corcoran
et al. (1988), after studying working conditions in urban schools, concluded that physical conditions have direct positive and negative effects on teacher morale, sense of personal safety, feelings of effectiveness in the classroom, and the general learning environment. While
building renovations in one district led teachers to feel hopeful that the
staff at the district office cared about the school, dilapidated buildings
in another district led to more despair and frustration, with teachers reporting that leaking roofs and burned-out lights were the typical back-
drop for teaching. Corcoran also found that if the problems with working conditions were severe enough to impinge on the work of teachers,
they resulted in higher absenteeism, lower levels of effort, lower effectiveness in the classroom, low morale, and reduced job satisfaction. It
seems fair to say that many teachers are expected to work in what
amounts to unfair working conditions where the buildings are in disrepair, they have larger-than-normal class size with a huge span of control, and they have to be concerned for their safety. A Carnegie Foundation report (1988) on urban schools concluded that the tacit message
for the physical indignities in many urban schools is not lost on students. It suggests neglect, and students' conduct seems simply an ex-
tension of the physical environment that surrounds them. The message
is not lost on teachers either. [5]

CONCLUSION

The poor condition of school facilities is a serious problem in America, particularly in the inner cities where space for construction is at

a premium and funding for such construction is limited. Crowded classroom conditions not only make it difficult for students to learn, but also limit the amount of time teachers can spend on nontraditional methods of teaching that may require additional materials and equipment. Much of the funding for improving these conditions has to be found in local communities, so the same issues of inequity and inadequacy that occur when considering the entire financial system for schools abound. Through bonded indebtedness programs, school districts are statutorily permitted to incur debt for long-term capital projects. The process depends on whether school districts are formally dependent on other units of government, such as a county, or are able to independently issue bonds. Although there is no definitive proof of correlation between quality of facilities and student learning and achievement, there has to be some link between lack of equipment and poor working conditions and student performance, as well as teacher satisfaction.

Localities generally finance construction and repair, with states playing varying roles and federal programs providing some money to help localities offset the impact of federal activities. These programs rarely offset the costs. The courts have long recognized the importance of facilities in the equity equation but states have not been able to improve the situation by either traditional or more innovative means, because the wealth of the local school district is still a disequilibrating factor. The role of the principal as the on-site leader is more challenging under these circumstances.

SUMMARY

- The inadequacy and the state of disrepair of school facilities have been addressed in many court cases on school finance since the mid-seventies. In most states, funding for facilities is provided from local sources, but there are built-in inequities in the provision of these monies. The federal government provided special funds following a report in 1996 from the General Accounting Office, where it was shown that many schools did not have the infrastructure to support the best use of computers.

- Various methods of funding—from long-term debt for school facilities (because the capital outlay is much more than can be financed through current revenue) to saving funds from current revenue over a period of time—were mentioned in this chapter.
- The role of the principal in the process is key throughout the various stages of needs analysis, planning for a new school, or renovating and upgrading existing facilities.
- Also addressed in this chapter was the issue of the importance of school facilities in the teaching/learning arena.

DISCUSSION ITEMS

1. You are the principal of a high school and you have to set up a sports evening for students in the exceptional educational program. Estimate additional costs involved in ensuring that all policies and regulations are met.
2. What are the advantages and disadvantages to using debt to finance capital outlay? What other methods can you suggest?
3. Interview an insurance representative about insuring a school that is over forty years old.

CHAPTER 7

The Politics of Education

The most important political move a principal can make is to graduate increasing proportions of students from elementary, middle, and high schools with an ever-improving quality of education, which will serve students well for each next level and ultimately for life in the greater society. Public schools in America were designed as the microcosm of the larger society to prepare students to be worthy citizens in a free society where a good education is the basis of freedom. Such a political move on the part of the principal can only produce positive results for all parties concerned. Administration of public schools does not occur in a vacuum; since schools are an integral part of the community, they are subject to political influences within the immediate community and those outside of the community. Principals need to have operational knowledge of the politics of education in order to succeed individually and as custodians of public trust. Kimbrough and Nunnery (1988) state that political power must be acquired to ensure that children and youth obtain quality education. The authors discuss the importance of the community, the board of education, and the politics of the bureaucracy.

The politics of the community is seen as important in several ways, including legitimizing educational programs in the schools and getting local financial support through the election process. Knowledge of community politics is even more important today, when local financial support through property taxes is losing the support of an aging population. Data on the age distribution of the resident population show that where the age group over fifty-five years represented 16.9 percent in the year 2000, by 2020, this group will comprise 25.4 percent of the total

Table 7.I Population projections by age: percent of total, years 2000–2020

Year	45–54 years	55 and older
2000	13.6	16.9
2005	14.7	18.6
2010	15.2	21.1
2020	12.3	25.4

Source: U. S. Department of Commerce (1993)

population—a change of 8.5 percent; the percentage increase for the forty-five to fifty-four years age group is −1.3 percent.

Many citizens who no longer have children in the school system may have difficulty supporting the rising cost of education through property taxes or by voting on school bond issues when they have to bear the cost in one way or the other. It is essential that the principal determine the sources of power within the community and the power bridges to political decision making, because educational policy involves the use of power at the school board level and beyond. Board members are drawn from the community; therefore, the politics of the community will be reflected in board actions and policies. As Iannaccone and Leitz (1970) put it, board members may be drawn into responsiveness to the ruling group in the community rather than to the school—so aligning school needs with community satisfaction is part of sound planning. On the other hand, the literature includes the view that school boards tend to drift toward elitism, stability, and some ignoring of citizens' demands (Kimbrough and Nunnery 1988). Over time, this situation allows for a widening gap between the board and the community. The principal's action can reflect awareness of the political climate between the community and the board for effectiveness at the individual school level.

POLITICS OF SCHOOL FINANCE

Decisions regarding the financing of public schools are political—they are made in accordance with specific political rules and regulations. Political decisions are unique in that these decisions require interaction, intermingling, and the agreement of many political actors and agencies.

These decisions are binding on all members of the political jurisdiction involved, even those who disagree with the decision. The general public can affect educational finance decisions by voting for school board members and state legislators, and by voting on school-related initiatives in referenda. When school boards are not elected, citizens can influence the political process by recommending potential appointees.

The public world of educational practice is a world of rules imposed on the schools by local, state, and federal authorities (Yudof et al. 1992). Yet the principal, as chief administrator at the individual school level, has some discretionary power in implementing the rules and regulations. If principals and teachers do not diffuse the political problems through their own strategies, then the authorities at the district level and above are likely to adopt formal rules. Political power of the principal is weak at best, and nonexistent at worst, unless the principal can function within the school's community to develop an efficient political machine that will articulate the needs of, and present workable solutions for, students in the individual school. In writing on the politics of inequality, Alexander and Salmon (1995) stated that a theory of redistribution politics in education must recognize that although each person has one vote, the significance and power of each vote is not equal, even after reapportionment. They see a lack of political power in those who are poor and live in low-wealth school districts.

Schools are designed to be public democratic organizations and are therefore operated through a political process to achieve their goals. Politics permeates all decisions in school finance. However, as the political machinery of the United States developed, so did the special interest groups that seem to be a natural outcome of the democratic society. Adam Smith (1937) noted in *The Wealth of Nations* that when an individual promotes his or her own interests, then the public interest is also promoted. If this is so, had school finance systems been truly democratic, there should be less inequality. Schlesinger (1991) commented on the fragmentation of the central values on which the United States was founded into ethnic, cultural, linguistic, religious, and nationalistic factions; that is, the democratic principles and process which should be uniting according to Locke ([1690] 1980) are being used to protect group rights rather than the individual rights intended to be protected by the Constitution.

Johns and Kimbrough (1968) suggest that in order to communicate effectively given local political processes, local administrators and principals should become aware of the community power structure and identify the values, goals, and beliefs of the different groups within it; communicate with the influential people in the power structure—parent groups, taxpayers, teacher organizations, labor unions, and other community groups—to provide opportunities for these groups to communicate with the school board; and provide information on school finance to these groups and the community as a whole, basing presentations on the educational level of the community involved (Kimbrough and Nunnery 1988).

TYPES OF COMMUNITY POWER STRUCTURE

Shively (1994) discusses different aspects of power within a community by making the distinction between formal and informal power structures. Formal power is seen as the machinery encompassing the elected officials, appointed officials, civic leaders, and other such groups. Informal power, on the other hand, lies with the people of the town who have status, wealth, expertise, and/or charisma. The three types of power structures referred to by Shively are totalitarian (where all segments of the community are run by a single power source), segmented power (which involves two or more power groups sharing power), and modified segmented power (which emerges during a crisis and requires groups to work together to resolve the issue). Further, over time, there can emerge a clustered segmented power structure that has a central core and that must relate to smaller influential groups who are major players in the community.

Johns and Kimbrough (1968) also identified four types of power structures found in school districts: monopolistic, multigroup noncompetitive, competitive elite, and democratic pluralism. Monopolistic structures occur where decision making and community policy development are dominated by a single group of leaders or a coalition of groups. This domination is seen as strong enough to stifle viable conflicts in community living. Multigroup noncompetitive structure exists where several important power groups participate in decision making.

The leaders of these groups are in basic agreement on issues concerning policy for schools. Competitive elite structure has been defined by Dye and Zeigler (1972) as a pluralism of elites, where cliques dominate the groups involved and participation by the general public is minimal. The community itself is seen as being in the middle of a power struggle concerning the kind of community it should be. Democratic pluralism structure occurs where there is widespread participation of the citizens of the school district in decision making. Decision making is open and governed by a common democratic ideology. Dahl (1961) sees pluralism as providing open access to decision making by persons and groups with little latent power because a high percentage of the people in the community participates. Here, organized interest groups are seen as important to the pluralistic structure.

Archer (1984) states that since political manipulation is the paramount in decision making and in creating change in a centralized system, then the social distribution of power is important in educational politics. In the case of a decentralized system, processes of negotiation can serve to balance power and shape educational politics. Elmore (1993) suggested that the reform debate on centralization and decentralization in education is really about power and its distribution. Garvue (1969) states that in a democracy, there is theoretically a high degree of control of the nonleaders over governmental leaders, and leaders must be drawn from the community-at-large rather than from a few social strata. Leadership is seen as being selected from a broad base and depends on active support of the community. Garvue also makes the point that, at the local level, the "local leeway of diversity" is a major factor in the relationship between local leadership and state administrators of education. Local leeway of diversity refers to the discretionary power in matters of finance, teachers, welfare, curriculum, staffing, and organization, thus allowing local administrators and principals to develop and operate educational programs of quality consistent with the community expectations, financial capability, and state fiscal policy. All this seems to be borne out by a finding in the 1995 Phi Delta Kappa/Gallup Poll of the Public's Attitude (Elam and Roise 1995) toward the public schools that people continue to rate the schools in their own communities much higher than they rate the nation's schools, with 65 percent of public school parents assigning a grade of

A or B to the school their oldest child attends. The reports from this poll showed a consistently high rating by communities for their schools, even though the percentage of parents with children in school fell from 41.5 percent in 1974 to 27 percent in 1995.

Regardless of the type of community power structure, certain truths will hold true. Leadership in the school and community plays a key role in fostering parent, family, and community involvement. Leaders set the tone for involvement, make it a priority, and provide the context that enables school personnel, families, community members, and businesspeople to maintain an active role in the education process. Schools need to look for a whole array of community connections; use creative approaches in defining leadership, designing programs, and solving problems; and provide a climate for success that includes making fiscal and human resources available. Communities should take an active role in making connections with schools. Families can represent the interests of children, and they can use community connections to advocate for the school. Leadership can be seen as going beyond the boundaries of the school and into the community (Rutherford and Billig 1995).

EDUCATION REFORM

A review of the education finance reform movement shows that perhaps the greatest fear preventing systemic education finance reform is the loss of local control. Although legal responsibility of education rests with the state, it is the local authorities who have been functionally responsible for education. As far back as the 1787 Northwest Ordnance, states and territories were expected to fund schools and were given the opportunity to use federally granted lands to provide support for schools (Thompson et al. 1994). Local school districts, despite their lack of legal authority, are still the basic unit of educational management and administration in America. The question must then be whether reform would weaken local control. Representatives from wealthy districts will favor local control while those from low-wealth districts may be willing to relinquish some control for additional state funds. A case in point is the reform in Michigan. If equity in funding is a goal, then in removing school district lines, the state of Michigan has taken the first real step toward systemic education finance reform. As Coons, Clune, and Sugarman mentioned in 1970, so long as school district lines coincide with neighborhood lines of division and the local property taxing effort is part of the school funding formula, there will be inequities in funding. The fiscal neutrality sought by students and their parents will not be achieved. Equity for taxpayers will also not be attained because property-poor districts generally must levy higher rates to raise an amount equal to that raised in property-rich districts. It is an indictment on state governments that the discussion in 1998 was still about education finance reform in general, and equity and adequacy of funding schools in particular.

States have not been consistent in funding innovations in all schools and have created inequities through matching funds programs. In fact, states have not focused on the end (that is, funding schools adequately) and instead have focused on the means of funding. To show commitment to reform, states need to develop state-of-the-art schools statewide; provide necessary, current textbooks statewide; commit to providing schools with teachers who have teaching time in their workday, as well as the supplies to do their jobs, across the state; ensure that pupil/teacher ratios across the state are low or at least at a level allowing for high-quality learning to take place; and ensure that students with special needs are satisfied without being dependent on the wealth of their school district. A relatively uncomplicated approach utilizes local property taxes as the basis of a minimum support program that requires all taxpayers in the state to be assessed a uniform levy. Amounts not raised by local tax efforts are supplemented by the state through other tax revenues. Money allocated on a weighted formula adds to the equity program (Burrup et al. 1996). Another case in point is provided by New Mexico, where the state assumed virtually full responsibility for school finance while retaining the district as the operating unit (Swanson and King 1997). No discretion is allowed to school districts in setting tax rates or determining revenues.

NEW ISSUES

President George W. Bush included several existing issues in his educational proposal for the nation; however, they can be seen as new issues only due to the change in emphasis brought by the change in the administration. The proposal included the following issues: testing to measure progress using the National Assessment of Educational Process as the benchmark; rewarding success and sanctioning failure using the accountability models present in many states; more options for parents by allowing portability of Title 1 funds for disadvantaged students in schools that fail to make adequate progress in three consecutive years; and funding to assist charter schools with start-up costs, facilities, and other needs. The proposal also creates a school-choice fund to demonstrate, develop, and provide information about innovative approaches that promote school choice; funding for research-based reading programs, including programs for Head Start; flexibility for states and charter districts to loosen the requirements for categorical program requirements under a five-year accountability program; and funding for teacher quality development through training and innovative programs, including reforming teacher certification, tenure, and merit-based performance systems (http://www.washingtonpost.com).

New issues in education reform have also risen from changes in several states as each adjusts equalization efforts to meet court mandates and consumer demands. Geotz and Derbertin (1992) report that in assessing revenue equalization under Kentucky reform, they found that funds available to all school districts had increased. The relationship between per pupil spending and the percentage of students living in poverty was reduced, and the previously high correlations between per pupil revenues and tax rates, achievement scores, economic deprivation, and per capita income had also gone down. The short-term success of the reform was attributed to the redefinition of allocation units from classrooms to individual students and to the incorporation into the funding formula of an allowance for pupils from economically deprived backgrounds.

Another emerging issue is school choice. School choice for families removes the underlying assumption of education finance reform—that is, students only attend the school in their residential district. Different districts spend different amounts, and with an open enrollment policy, costs have to be viewed differently. For example, transportation costs for a given district could change if even one student attends school outside the residential district. If students leave a low-achieving, low-wealth district for a high achieving, high-wealth district, should the student's per pupil amount be increased or can the state only provide funding at the minimum education level? In 1999, 63 percent of classrooms in the nation's public schools had Internet access—up from 30 percent in 1994. However, where 39 percent of classrooms in high-poverty areas had access in 1998, 62 percent of classrooms in low-poverty areas had access (National Center for Education Statistics 2001).

Reform has to be systemic. Increasing funding to continue business as usual in the same school structure is not systemic reform. As Hanushek (1996) observed, new resources being absorbed by old, failing structures are not being allocated to the programmatic innovations shown to improve student performance. In order to improve performance, there have to be changes in the incentive structure. The issue of reform is now moving from concern over the equitable treatment of institutions to the equitable treatment of individuals. Wang (1994) maintained that the lack of progress in achieving equity in the provision of resources is the result of different focuses at federal, state, and local levels. Federal policy has focused on special needs student population, the state has focused on equalizing interdistrict fiscal capacity, and the local district has concentrated on giving each teacher an equal number of students. This functional fragmentation has not been conducive to equity.

SYSTEMIC REFORM

Systemic reform means (1) determining students' needs and making every effort to meet them; this is crucial in the current climate of inclusion where the needs of the regular student population may be subverted by those of the special-needs student in the classroom at each grade level, and (2) providing high-quality curriculum with meaningful evaluation procedures that would lead to improved learning opportunities. The focus could be on the impact of curriculum on the student and not on the numbers of students passing examinations. With existing and proposed technology, it could be easy to establish tutorial laboratories to help students learn—not to improve grades but to *learn* at each level to advance to the next. Inequities can only exacerbate the problem of building an underclass if not addressed in conjunction with curriculum planning.

Providing high-quality remuneration for teachers, including improved working conditions, is another issue to be considered. Both teachers and students will benefit from smaller class sizes and a safe and disciplined environment. Other possibilities include providing teachers with more teaching time and fewer nonteaching duties, providing a learning climate that will benefit both teacher and students, funding improved professional development programs for teachers and administrators at the school level, or funding community-based programs to fully include parents in the teaching/learning environment.

More attention can be paid to differences within the district and within the level. Berne and Stiefel (1996) found that teachers' salaries in high-poverty subdistricts in New York City were lower than in low-poverty subdistricts. Poorer students were taught by less-experienced teachers who were paid at a lower rate, thus suggesting that allocation of teacher resources should be an integrated part of education finance reform. Jones and Chavis (1999) found evidence of intradistrict inequities in North Carolina that had not been addressed when poor school districts were merged with wealthy districts, such that the whole was fragmented in needs and use of resources.

Funding must continue to be provided so that schools are accessible to homeless children and their parents. In recognition of the special needs of homeless children and youths, Congress passed the McKenney Act (42 U.S.C. Sec.11301 West Supp. 1993) in 1987 to respond to the critically urgent needs of the homeless, including the proper education of their children. The act calls for such measures as continuing the homeless child's education at the child's original school and providing each homeless child with services comparable to those offered to other students in the school.

Molnar (1995) stated,

> Our constitutional values require that each child have an equal claim on whatever resources we provide for public education. In practical terms this means spending at least as much money on children living in poverty as we spend on their wealthier brothers and sisters. To spend enough to buy a Cadillac education for some children while others must settle for a used Chevette is an obvious affront to our constitutional principles. It reflects the decision to treat some children as more valuable than others.

Unfortunately, the current debate over education spending often manages to obscure this simple truth. (58)

Choice, open enrollment, charter schools, vouchers, privatization, and increased home schooling have generated a lot of debate over the last few years, signaling that the established, traditional order of things has been challenged and found wanting by all interested parties. The jury is still out on solutions.

SITE-BASED MANAGEMENT

Reference has been made several times in this book to the principal as the site-based manager, with the inference that the principal can make a difference from this unique position. Site-based management programs are a way to structure school site/district relationship in a manner that places much more power, authority, and accountability in the schools. These programs were originally proposed as a way to help schools produce higher student achievement (North Carolina Regional Laboratory 2000). Bailey (1997) points out that there is no one site-based management model to fit all schools. Further, it is a method for obtaining better decisions and nothing more. Site-based management programs have also been seen as a means of getting more efficient use of resources, increased skills and satisfaction of school administrators and teachers, and greater community and business involvement in support of schools. Some dissenters feel that a mere change in the structure of school management cannot achieve these goals unless there is concomitant change in budget control and spending. Whalstetter and Odden (1992) showed that up until 1990, site-based management programs did not allow for decentralization of significant portions of the budget or improve student achievement. Even in states where accountability models for student achievement and teacher monitoring have been put in place, there is still no real change in control of funds at the school level. Yet, according to Bailey (1991), even while it may be complicated, many decisions can be made at the building level, and there are several methods of assigning rudimentary budget decisions to the schools. He suggests that the secret is to have flexibility within the various items in the budget. Funds for instructional supplies and materials, equipment, faculty maintenance and improvement, student activities, assemblies, and field trips can all be managed more effectively at the building level. Perhaps the closest example of flexibility in spending is provided in charter schools' structures, but the methods are so varied that it is difficult at this time to categorize spending patterns in charter schools across the nation. Geortz and Odden (1999) felt that the funding devolution could help improve not only the effectiveness of the spending of education dollars but also the effectiveness of the entire education system involved in efficient site-based management.

PRINCIPALS AS CHANGE LEADERS

Drucker (1999) wrote, "being a change leader requires the willingness and ability to change what is *already* being done just as much as the ability to do new and different things. It requires policies and practices that make the present and create the future" (65). He continues to say that the first step for a change leader is to free up resources that are committed to maintaining things that no longer contribute to performance and no longer produce results. Doing something different demands leadership; if people are committed to maintaining yesterday, they are simply not available to create tomorrow. Although this view may seem more appropriate for a business organization, the concept of a change agent is part of the leadership persona of educational administrators, and certainly of principals who are heading organizations serving children. The principal is constantly working with the future; if using the limited power structure is not enough to manage change, and since change is inevitable, why not lead it?

Principals need to play a crucial leadership role in developing schools, lobbying for smaller schools, and getting to know their students and staff. In a typical management scenario, the managerial span is eight to ten individuals, yet school principals are asked to supervise and lead 1800 students at times. To do this, superintendents and school boards must provide them with the professional development, especially in developing technology skills, and the other support required to carry out their leadership roles effectively in a site-based management setting. Perhaps changing the nature of school litigation, whereby some empowerment is transferred to the school level so that each school can become a learning environment, is the reform effort needed. Parental involvement must become more than the latest catch phrase. Involvement for parents need not be so much of participation in governance, but in ensuring that the interests of parents for their children are voiced, considered in decision making, and not taken for granted. The principal is in a unique position to interface with parents and address their concerns and interests. Of particular concern are the parents in low-income communities. Parents who lack wealth or knowledge themselves do not necessarily lack interest in the schools their children attend. The race of the parent and the student must be acknowledged as a factor in parental involvement policy in schools. Statistics have shown the parents of minority races have not been given equal standing in schools. The real issue is power, which in the case of education has been increasingly concentrated in the hands of a few who may not want radical change—hence the nation is still at risk (Office of Educational Research 1999).

SUMMARY

- The politics of the community is seen as very important to principals because knowledge of this element can only help in providing local financial support for schools. Schools exist in a world where the rules affecting them are made at local, state, and federal levels and where long-term goals are developed, but these goals have to be implemented by the school principal at the building level.
- Four types of community structures were identified: monopolistic, multigroup noncompetitive, competitive elite, and democratic pluralism.
- Education reform is reviewed in the light of school finance structures and the loss of local control, which dates at least as far back as 1787 with the passage of the Northwest Ordinance. Part of the literature on education reform addresses the area of systemic reform, which requires radical changes in all sectors.
- Site-based management is seen as a unique position from which the principal can be a change leader.

DISCUSSION ITEMS

1. As principal, you have to hire five new teachers, but the local supplement is providing funds for only three new teachers. Provide rationale for obtaining more money to fund the other two positions. Alternatively, develop a plan that would accommodate only three teaching positions.
2. Prepare a political narrative to accompany budget requests to the school board for the next three school years.
3. Develop an outline for a paper on the direction that you think school finance reform will take in the twenty-first century.
4. Find four school districts in your state whose power structures approximate those mentioned in the chapter. Provide a clear picture of the characteristics that made you select these districts.

References

Adams, J. E. 1928. A study in the equalization of educational opportunities in Kentucky. *Bulletin of the University of Kentucky* 20 (September), 256.

Alexander, K., and R. G. Salmon. 1995. *Public school finance*. Needham Heights, Mass.: Allyn & Bacon.

Annan, K. 2000. Annan underscores education for all girls. *Daily News*. [accessed 26 January 2001: http://newafrica.com]

Archer, D. S. 1984. *Social origins of educational systems*. London: Sage.

Association of Supervision and Curriculum Development. 1999. *Financing schools equitably: An infobrief synopsis*. [accessed 1 June 1999: http://www.ascd.org/issue/finance.html]

Auerbach, C. A., L. K. Garrison, and W. M. S. Hurst. 1961. *The legal process*. San Francisco: Chandler.

Bailey, W. J. 1991. *School-site management applied*. Lancaster, Pa.: Technomic.

——. 1997. *Organizing schools*. Lancaster, Pa.: Technomic.

Baldwin, R. D. 1927. *Financing rural education*. Stevens Point, Wisc.: Rural Press.

Bartizol, J. R. 1942. *Budget principles and procedures*. Englewood Cliffs, N.J.: Prentice Hall.

Becker, G. S. 1964. *Human capital: A theoretical and empirical analysis with special reference to education*. New York: National Bureau of Economic Research.

Berg, I. 1969. *Education and jobs: The great training robbery*. New York: Praeger Press.

Berne, R., and L. Stiefel. 1984. *The measurement of equity in school finance: Conceptual methodological and empirical dimensions*. Baltimore, Md.: John Hopkins University Press.

———. 1994. Measuring equity at the school level: The finance perspective. *Educational Evaluation and Policy Analysis* 16, 405–421.

Bernstein, A. 1994. Inequality: How gaps between rich and poor hurt the economy. *Business Week* (August 15), 47.

Boyette, J. H., and H. P. Conn. 1991. *Workplace 2000: The revolution reshaping American business*. New York: Dulton.

Burnett, G. 1995. *Overcrowding in urban schools*. ERIC/CUE Digest No.107. New York: ERIC Clearinghouse on Urban Education. ERIC Document Reproduction Service No. ED 384 682.

Burrup, P. E., V. Brimley Jr., and R. R. Garfield. 1996. *Financing education in a climate of change*. 6th ed. Boston, Mass.: Allyn & Bacon

Busch, R. J., and D. O. Stewart. 1992. Voters' opinion of school district property taxes and income taxes: Results from an exit-poll in Ohio. *Journal of Education Finance* 17 (spring), 337–351.

Candoli, I. C., W. G. Hack, and J. R. Ray. 1992. *School business administration: A planning approach*. 4th ed. Boston, Mass.: Allyn & Bacon.

Carnegie Foundation for the Advancement of Teaching. 1988. *An imperiled generation: Saving urban schools*. Princeton, N.J.: Carnegie Foundation. ERIC Document Reproduction Service No. ED 293 940.

Clotfelter, C. T., and P. J. Cook. 1989. *Selling hope: State lotteries in America*. Cambridge, Mass.: Harvard University Press.

Coons, J. E., W. H. Clune, and S. D. Sugarman. 1970. *Private wealth and public education*. Cambridge, Mass.: Harvard University Press.

Corcoran, T. B., L. J. Walker, and J. L. White. 1988. *Working in urban schools*. Washington, D.C.: Institute for Educational Leadership.

Cumberland County Schools. 1994. *Accounting procedures for the individual school funds*. Fayetteville, N.C.: Cumberland County Schools.

Cuzzetto, C. 1995. Student activity funds creating a system of controls that work. *School Business Affairs* 61, 18–22.

Dahl, R. A. 1961. *Who governs?* New Haven, Conn.: Yale University Press.

Dewey, J. 1902. *The school and society*. Chicago, Ill.: University of Chicago Press.

Drucker, P. F. 1999. Change leaders. *Inc.* 21 (June), 64–66.

Dworkin, R. 1986. *A matter of principle*. Oxford: Clarendon Press.

Dye, T. R., and L. H. Zeigler. 1972. *The irony of democracy*. Belmont, Calif.: Duxbury Press.

Earthman, G., C. Cash, and D. Van Berkem. 1995. September. A statewide study of student achievement and behavior and school building condition. Paper presented at the annual meeting of the Council of Educational Facility Planners International. Dallas, Tex. ED387878.

Education Commission of the States. 1998. *Finance: Litigation*. [accessed 9 October 1999: http://www.ecs.org/ecs/ecsweb.nsf/31696]

——. 2000. *Selected state policies: Finance-equity*. [accessed 12 January 2001, http://www.ecs.org].

Elam, S. M., and L. C. Roise. 1995. Of the public's attitudes toward the public schools. *Phi Delta Kappa* (September), 41–46.

Elmore, R. F. 1993. School decentralization. Who gains? Who loses? In *Decentralization and school improvement*, edited by J. Hannaway and M. Carnoy. San Francisco: Jossey-Bass.

Englehart, F., and F. von Borgerarode. 1927. *Accounting procedures for school systems*. New York: Bureau of Publications, Teachers College Columbia University.

Everett, R. E., R. L. Lows, and D. R. Johnson. 1996. *Financial and managerial accounting for school administrators*. Reston, Va.: Association of School Business Officials Intl.

Freedman, M. 1955. The role of government in education. In *Economic and the public intent*, edited by Robert Solo. New Brunswick, N.J.: Rutgers University Press.

Garms, W. I., J. W. Guthrie, and L. C. Pierce. 1978. *School finance: The economics and politics of public education*. Englewood Cliffs, N.J.: Prentice Hall.

Garvue, R. J. 1969. *Modern public school finance*. London: Macmillan.

General Accounting Office. 2000. *Charter schools limited access to facility financing*. [accessed 12 September 2000: http://www.gao.gov].

Geortz, M. E., and A. Odden, eds. 1999. *School-based financing*. Thousand Oaks, Calif.: Corwin.

Geotz, S., and D. L. Derbertin. 1992. Rural areas and education reform in Kentucky: An early assessment of resource equalization. *Journal of Education Finance* 18, 163–179.

Ginzberg, E. 1964. *The house of Adam Smith*. New York: Oregon Books.

Governmental Accounting Standards Board. 1987/1990. Codification of governmental accounting and financial reporting standards. Stamford, Conn.: Governmental Accounting Standards Board, Sec. 1100.102.

——. 2000. *Facts about GASB*. [accessed 20 December 2000: http://accounting.rugers.edu].

Grossnickle, F. E. 1931. *Capital outlay in relation to a state's minimum educational program*. New York: Teachers College, Columbia University. Teachers College Contributions to Education no. 464. 67.

Hack, W. G., I. C. Candoli, and J. R. Ray. 1998. *School business administration*. 6th ed. Boston, Mass.: Allyn and Bacon.

Hanushek, E. A. 1994. A jaundiced view of "adequacy" in school finance reform. *Educational Policy* 8, 460–469.

———. 1996. Measuring investment in education. *Journal of Economic Perspectives* 10, 9–30.

———. 1997. Applying performance incentives to schools for disadvantaged populations. *Education & Urban Schools* 29, 296–316.

Harley, J. M., and S. Zuckerman. *Health insurance access and use: United States.* [accessed 20 December 2000: http://www.urban.org].

Hartman, W. T. 1988. *School district budgeting.* Englewood Cliff, N.J.: Prentice-Hall.

Herman, J. J., and J. L. Herman. 1997. *School-based budgets: Getting spending and accounting.* Lancaster, Pa.: Technomic.

Hess, G. A. 1995. School-based finance: An equity solution for urban schools. *School Business Affairs* 61, 34–38.

Hodgkinson, H. L. 1985. *All one system: Demographics of education, kindergarten through graduate school.* Washington, D.C.: Institute for Educational Leadership.

Hornbeck, D. W., and L. M. Salmon, eds. 1991. *Human capital and America's future.* Baltimore, Md.: Johns Hopkins University Press.

Hosteller, A. J. 1994. CDC study finds high health cost of poor education. *Daily Herald* (December 15), 4.

Hunt, E. 1995. *Will we be smart enough? A cognitive analysis of the coming workforce.* New York: Russell Sage Foundation.

Hunter, F. 1953. *Community power structure.* Chapel Hill: University of North Carolina Press.

Iannaccone, L., and F. W. Lutz. 1970. *Politics, power and policy: The governing of school districts.* Columbus, Ohio: Merrill.

ILO Washington Focus. 1995. Quoted in "Income distribution." *Too Much Newsletter* 1 (spring), 2.

Johns, R. L., and R. B. Kimbrough. 1968. *The relationship of socioeconomic factors, educational leadership patterns, and elements of community power structure to local school fiscal policy.* Final Report, Office of Education Cooperative Research Project No. 2842. Washington, D.C.: Department of Health Education and Welfare.

Jones, E. B., and M. Chavis. 1999. Are there savage inequalities in Robeson County, NC? Paper presented at the meeting of the American Education Finance Association, Seattle, Wash.

Jones, T. H. 1985. *Introduction to school finance: Technique and social policy.* New York: Macmillan.

Jordan, K. F. 1985. *School business administration.* Beverly Hills, Calif.: Sage.

Jordan, K. F., and T. S. Lyons. 1992. *Financing public education in an era of change*. Bloomington, Ind.: Phi Delta Kappa Educational Foundation.

Judge critical of states education funding system. 2000. Fayetteville Observer, 13 October. [accessed 13 October 2000: http://www.fayettevillenc.com].

Kickbush, P. 1996. *The President's School Construction Initiative*. [accessed in 1999: www.listserve edinfo@inet.ed.gov]

Kimbrough, R. B., and M. Y. Nunnery. 1988. *Educational administration: An introduction*. 3rd ed. New York: Macmillan.

Kozol, J. 1992. *Savage inequalities: Children in America's schools*. New York: Harper Perennial.

Lindman, E. L. 1948. *The development of an equalized matching formula for the apportionment of state school building aid*. Seattle: University of Washington Press.

Locke, J. [1690] 1980. *Second treatise of government*. Indianapolis, Ind.: Hackett.

McGuffey, C. 1982. Facilities. In *Improving educational standards and productivity*, edited by Herver Walberg. Berkeley, Calif.: McCutchan.

McKinsey and Company. 1995. *Connecting K–12 schools to the information superhighway*. Palo Alto, Calif.: McKinsey and Company.

McLaughlin, M. W. 1987. Involving low-income parents in the schools: A role for policy? *Phi Delta Kappan* 69 (October), 156–160.

Molnar, A. 1995. School funding: The right issue, the wrong logic. *Educational Leadership* 33, 58–59.

Morrison, H. C. 1930. *School revenue*. Chicago, Ill.: University of Chicago Press.

National Center for Education Statistics. 1967. *Principles of public school accounting*. Washington, D.C.: GPO.

———. 1990. *Financial accounting for local and state school systems 1990*. Washington, D.C.: U. S. Department of Education.

———. 1993. *Digest of Education Statistics 1992*. Washington, D.C.: U.S. Department of Education.

———. 1997. *Digest of Education Statistics 1996*. Washington, D.C.: U.S. Department of Education.

———. 1997. *Federal support for education: Fiscal years 1980 to 1997*. NCES 97-383. Washington, D.C.: U.S. Department of Education

———. 1997. *Statistical analysis report: Early labor force experiences and debt burden*. [accessed 26 September 1998: http://nces.ed.gov./pub 97/97286.html]

———. 1998. *Digest of Education Statistics 1997*. Washington, D.C.: GPO.

———. 1999. *School finance litigation case citations*. [accessed 4 December 1999: http://nces.ed.gov/edfin/Litigation/Citation.asp]

——. 2000. *Digest of Education Statistics 1999*. Washington, D.C.: U.S. Department of Education.

——. 2001. *Internet access in U.S. public schools and classrooms: 1994-2000*. [accessed 20 March 2000: http://www.nces.ed.gov/pubs2001].

North Carolina 1997. *State auditor: Types of government audits*. [accessed 10 July 1998: http://www.osa.state.nc.us/OAS/yellow/ybchap2.htm]

North Carolina Department of Public Instruction. 1996. *Policy Allotment Manual 1996*. Raleigh: N.C. Department of Public Instruction.

——. 2000. *Public Schools of North Carolina: Statistical Profile 2000*. [accessed 26 January 2001: http:www.ncpublicschools.org/stat/stats200.html].

North Carolina Regional Educational Laboratory. 2000. *Implementing site-based management to support student achievement*. [accessed 20 December 2000: http://www.ncrel.org].

Odden, A. R., and L. O. Picus. 1992. *School finance: A policy perspective*. New York: McGraw-Hill.

Office of Educational Research and Improvement. 1999. *A nation still at risk*. 1999. College Park, Md.: Clearinghouse on Assessment and Evaluation. ERIC No. ERIC ED 429 988.

Parnes, H. S. 1984. *People power: Elements of human resource policy*. Beverly Hills, Calif.: Sage.

Parrish, T. B., and W. J. Fowler. 1995. *Disparities in public school district spending 1989–90*. Washington, D.C.: National Center for Education Statistics.

Pfeiffer, J. 1994. *Competitive advantage through people: Unleashing the power of the workforce*. Boston, Mass.: Harvard Business School Press.

Phillips, L. 1995. Welfare pit deep for uneducated. *USA Today* (March), A3.

Pipho, C. 1993. Taxes, politics, and education. *Phi Delta Kappan 65* (September), 6–7.

Reed, D. S. 1996. *Court-ordered school finance equalization: Judicial activism and democratic opposition. Developments in School Finance 1996*. NCES. [accessed 8 July: http://www.nces.ed.gov/pubs 97/97535g.html]

Reich, R. B. 1995. *Too Much Newsletter,* 10.

——. 2000. *The future of success*. New York: Knopf.

Rivera-Batiz, F. L., and L. Marti. 1995. *A school system at risk: A study of the consequences of overcrowding in New York City public schools*. New York: New York Institute for Urban and Minority Education, Columbia University.

Rogers, D., and N. H. Chung. 1983. *110 Livingston Street revisited*. New York: New York University Press

Romer, P. 1994. Inequality: How the gap between rich and poor hurts the economy. *Business Week* (August 15), 78.

Rutherford, B., and S. H. Billig. 1995. Parent, family and community involvement in the middle grades. Urbana, Ill.: ERIC Clearinghouse on Elementary and Early Childhood Education. ERIC No. ED387 273.

Schlesinger, A. M. 1991. *The disuniting of America*. Knoxville: Whittle Direct Books.

Shafritz, J. M. 1992. *The HarperCollins dictionary of American government and politics*. New York: Harper Perennial.

Sharp, W. L. 1994. *The principal as school manager*. Lancaster, Pa.: Technomic.

Shively, R. 1994. Community power structures. *Economic Development Review* 12: 13-16 [accessed 23 March 2000: http://ww.epnet.com/ehost/login.html].

Shively, W. P. 1997. *Power and choice: An introduction to political science*. New York: McGraw-Hill.

Shultz, T. W. 1961. Involvement in human capital. *America Economic Review* 51, 1–17.

———. 1981. *Investing in people: The economics of population quality*. Berkeley: University of California Press.

Smith, A. 1937. *The wealth of nations*. New York: Modern Library Edition.

Sparkman, W. E. 1990. School finance challenges in the courts. In *The impacts of litigation and legislation in public school finance*, edited by J. K. Underwood and D. C. Verstegen, 193–224. New York: Harper & Row.

Spring, J. 1984. The structure of power in an urban system: a study of Cincinnati school politics. *Curriculum Inquiry* 14 (winter), 401–424.

Stewart, T. A. 1997. *Intellectual capital: The new wealth of organizations*. New York: Doubleday.

Strayer, G. D., and R. N. Haig. 1923. *The financing of education in the state of New York, Report of the Educational Finance Inquiry Commission*, vol 1. New York: Macmillan.

Swanson, A. D., and R. A. King. 1997. *School finance: Its economics and politics*. 2nd ed. White Plains, N.Y.: Longman.

Thierauf, R. J. 1993. *Creative computer software for strategic thinking and decision making*. Westport, Conn.: Quorum Books.

Thompson, D. C., R. C. Wood, and D. S. Honeyman. 1994. *Fiscal leadership for schools: Concepts and practices*. White Plains, N.Y.: Longman Publishing Group.

Thornley, A., and J. Williams. 1997. *Investing in Society: Health, Education and Development*. [accessed 26 January 2001: http://www.acdi-cida.ge.ca/xpress]

Thorpe, F. N., ed. 1993. *The federal and state constitutions*. Buffalo, N.Y.: William S. Heinz.

U.S. Bureau of the Census. 1998. *Income inequality*. [accessed 28 September 1998: http://www.census.gov/ftp/pub/hes/income/ineq/p60tb.3.html].

———. 1998. *Dynamics of economic well-being: Health insurance statistics 1992 to 1994*. [accessed 28 September 1998: http;//www.census.gov/hhes/hlthins/hlth9293/hi93t6.html]

———. 1999. *Statistical abstract of the United States: 1999*. Washington, D.C.

U. S. Department of Commerce. 1993. *Statistical abstract of the United States*. Washington, D.C.

———. 1995. *Statistical abstract of the United States*. Washington, D.C.

———. 1997. *Statistical abstract of the United States*. Washington, D.C.

U.S. Department of Education. 1990. *National goals for education*. Washington, D.C.

———. 1996. *Goals 2000: Educate America Act, October 1996*. Update. [accessed 26 September 1998: http://inet.ed.gov/G2k/g2k-fact.html]

———. 1997. *Digest of Education Statistics*. National Center for Education Statistics. Washington, D.C.

———. 1999. *Digest of Education Statistics*. National Center for Education Statistics. Washington, D.C.

———. 2000. *Digest of Education Statistics*. National Center for Education Statistics. Washington, D.C.

———. 2000. *The federal role in education*. [accessed 10 March 2001: www.ed.gov/offices/OUS/fedrole.html].

U.S. General Accounting Office. 1995. *School facilities: America's schools not designed or equipped for 21st century*. Washington, D.C.

———. 1996. *School facilities: America's schools report differing conditions*. Washington, D.C.

———. 1997. *School facilities: reported condition and costs to repair schools funded by Bureau of Indian Affairs*. Washington, D.C.

———. 1998. *School finance: State and federal efforts to target poor students*. Washington, D.C.: Health Education and Human Services Division.

Updegraff, H. 1922. *Rural school survey of New York State*. Ithaca, N.Y.: William F. Fell.

Venn, J. R., and A. B. Weiss. 1993. *Education and the work histories of the young adults*. Washington, D.C.: U.S. Department of Labor, Bureau of Labor Statistics.

Wahlstetter, P., and A. R. Odden. 1992. Rethinking school-based management policy and research. *Educational Administration Quarterly* 28, 529–549.

Wang, K. K. 1994. Governance structure resource allocation and equity policy. *Review of Research in Education* 20, 257–289.

Wannacott, P., and R. Wannacott. 1979. *Economics*. New York: McGraw-Hill.

Weller, G. M. 1940. *State equalization of capital outlays for public school buildings*. Los Angeles: University of Southern California Press.

Whitney, T. 1994. School funding alternatives. *LegisBrief* 2, 23. Denver, Colo.: National Conference of State Legislatures.

Wirt, F. M., and M. W. Kirst. 1982. *The politics of education schools in conflict*. Berkeley, Calif.: McCutchan.

Wise, A. 1969. *Rich schools-poor schools: A study of equal educational opportunity*. Chicago, Ill.: University of Chicago Press.

Workforce 2000: Key trends. [accessed 26 September 1998: http://cbpa.louisville.edu/bruce/mgt601/diverse/tsld015.htm]

Yudof, M. G., D. L. Kirp, and B. Levin. 1992. *Educational policy and the law*. 3rd ed. St. Paul, Minn.: West Publishing.

Appendix A

Funding for public schools by level of government, 1996–1997 (in thousands of dollars)

State	Local Amount	% of total	State Amount	% of total	Federal Amount	% of total	Total no. of schools
Alabama	887,000	22.4	2,499,000	63.2	378,000	9.6	1,353
Alaska	270,000	22.2	773,000	63.4	144,341	11.8	497
Arizona	1,909,000	43.4	1,981,000	45.0	408,000	9.3	1,340
Arkansas	641,000	27.0	1,425,000	60.1	186,000	7.8	1,112
California	10,604,000	30.8	20,670,000	60.0	2,818,000	8.2	7,984
Colorado	1,910,000	47.2	1,788,000	44.19	212,000	5.2	1,562
Connecticut	2,776,000	56.7	1,817,000	37.1	170,000	3.5	1,080
Delaware	230,000	26.2	569,000	64.8	67,000	7.6	186
District of Columbia	633,000	89.0*	—	—	75,000	10.5	171
Florida	5,541,000	40.0	6,768,000	48.8	1022,000	7.4	2,888
Georgia	3,045,000	37.5	4,366,000	53.7	556,000	6.8	1,823
Hawaii	5,431	0.04	1,088,000	89.5	98,000	8.1	251
Idaho	351,000	28.1	795,000	63.5	84,000	6.7	642
Illinois	8,465,000	64.3	3,553,000	27.0	828,000	6.3	4,244
Indiana	3,257,000	42.6	3,854,000	50.5	318,000	4.2	1,926
Iowa	1,193,000	37.7	1,647,000	52.0	161,000	5.1	1,552
Kansas	1,081,000	35.6	1,708,000	56.2	170,000	5.6	1,454
Kentucky	993,000	26.2	2,387,000	62.9	351,000	9.3	1,418
Louisiana	1,478,000	35.6	2,088,000	50.3	485,000	11.7	1,488
Maine	706,000	47.1	708,000	47.2	81,000	5.4	724
Maryland	3,195,000	52.9	2,343,000	38.8	312,000	5.2	1,300
Massachusetts	3,903,000	54.0	2,883,000	39.9	347,000	4.8	1,868
Michigan	3,479,000	25.9	8,805,000	65.5	884,000	6.6	3,862
Minnesota	2,252,000	36.9	3,360,000	55.0	264,000	4.3	2,260
Mississippi	613,000	27.1	1,253,000	55.5	315,000	14.0	1,013

Funding for public schools by level of government, 1996–1997 (in thousands of dollars)

State	Amount	Local % of total	Amount	State % of total	Amount	Federal % of total	Total no. of schools
Missouri	2,774,000	49.8	2,247,000	40.3	330,000	5.9	2,301
Montana	387,846	39.0	470,000	47.4	93,000	9.4	899
Nebraska	1,103,000	56.4	627,000	32.1	117,000	6.0	1,375
Nevada	1,029,000	60.4	543,000	31.9	71,000	4.2	455
New Hampshire	1,111,000	86.6	95,000	7.4	44,000	3.5	413
New Jersey	6,886,000	55.6	4,793,000	38.7	434,000	3.5	2,314
New Mexico	222,000	12.2	1,337,000	73.1	232,000	12.7	745
New York	14,402,000	54.2	10,468,000	39.4	1,447,000	5.4	4,208
North Carolina	1,510,000	24.6	4,258,000	65.4	471,000	7.2	2,063
North Dakota	266,000	41.3	266,000	41.4	77,000	12.0	605
Ohio	6,187,000	49.2	5,126,000	40.7	768,000	6.1	3,945
Oklahoma	790,000	24.3	2,026,000	62.3	268,000	8.3	1,840
Oregon	1,300,000	37.4	1,826,000	52.6	216,000	6.2	1,253
Pennsylvania	7,731,000	53.5	5,653,000	39.1	788,000	5.5	3,181
Rhode Island	629,000	52.7	485,000	40.6	64,000	5.4	314
South Carolina	1,352,000	34.8	2,040,000	52.5	328,000	8.4	1,096
South Dakota	387,000	51.7	265,000	35.5	73,000	9.7	832
Tennessee	1,616,000	36.6	2,142,000	48.5	376,000	8.5	1,571
Texas	11,063,000	49.4	9,026,000	40.3	1,719,000	7.7	7,090
Utah	622,000	28.3	1,382,000	62.8	138,000	6.3	759
Vermont	527,000	64.9	223,000	28.6	38,000	4.6	395
Virginia	4,275,000	59.3	2,338,000	32.5	358,000	5.0	1,910
Washington	1,592,000	24.0	4,455,000	67.1	389,000	5.9	2,180
West Virginia	567,000	27.2	1,313,000	63.0	172,000	8.3	854
Wisconsin	2,715,000	40.5	3,557,000	53.1	288,000	4.3	2,112
Wyoming	283,000	43.1	319,000	48.5	43,000	6.6	413

Source: U.S. Department of Education 2000

Appendix B

State and local per pupil expenditure by selected school districts, North Carolina, 1998–1999

Ten wealthiest school districts	State	Local	State percent of total (including federal funds)
Chapel Hill-Carrboro	3,964	3,024	55
Asheville City	4,416	2,691	58
Durham County	4,460	2,212	62
Guilford County	3,976	1,640	67
Dare County	4,082	1,768	69
Forsyth County	4,073	1,712	68
Mecklenburg County	3,868	2,018	63
Orange County	4,143	2,229	67
Currituck County	4,375	1,736	69
Wake County	3,894	1,567	69
Ten poorest school districts			
Swain County	5,302	277	82
Hoke County	4,309	428	84
Alexander County	4,130	??	82
Cherokee County	4,909	646	81
Mitchell County	4,852	529	86
Washington County	5,094	741	79
Madison County	5,052	630	83
Robeson County	4,182	492	82
Harnett County	4,075	609	83

Source: N.C. Department of Public Instruction 2000

Appendix C

Example A. School district XYZ: combined balance sheet; all fund types and account groups, June 30, 20XX

Assets and other debits	Governmental fund types				Proprietary Fund types		Fiduciary Fund types	Account groups		Totals (memo-randum only)
	General	Special revenue	Debt service	Capital projects	Enter-prise	Internal service	Trust and agency	General fixed assets	General long-term debt	
Current assets:										
Cash	$56,050	$23,310	$34,210	$12,700	$76,090	$10,500	$5,620			$219,480
Cash with fiscal agents			92,000							92,000
Investments	215,000	65,000	132,000	419,000			270,000			1,101,000
Taxes receivable (net of allowances for estimated uncollectible, see notes to financial statements)	62,000	2,660	4,250							68,910
Interfund receivables	67,000			15,000	2,000	11,200	11,000			106,200
Intergovernmental receivables	30,000	75,260								105,260
Other receivables (net of allowances for estimated uncollectible, see notes to financial statements)	950				3,900					4,850
Bond proceeds receivable				10,000						10,000
Inventories	27,200	9,400		800	45,900	18,200				101,500
Prepaid expenses	32,500	21,300			1,480	1,480				66,760
Other current assets	12,200	900								13,100
Total current assets	502,900	206,830	262,460	457,500	131,370	41,380	286,620			1,089,060

Example A. Continued.

Assets and other debits	Governmental fund types				Proprietary Fund types		Fiduciary Fund types	Account groups		Totals (memorandum only)
	General	Special revenue	Debt service	Capital projects	Enter-prise	Internal service	Trust and agency	General fixed assets	General long-term debt	
Fixed assets:										
Sites								192,000		192,000
Site improvements (net of accumulated depreciation, $4,240)								39,260		39,260
Buildings (act of accumulated depreciation, $429,480)								3,994,320		3,994,320
Machinery and equipment (net of accumulated depreciation, see notes to financial statements)					52,050	54,950		709,080		816,080
Construction in progress							892,000			892,000
Total fixed assets					52,050	54,950	5,826,660			5,933,660
Other debits										
Amount available in debt service funds									169,710	169,710
Amount to be provided for retirement of general long-term debt									2,630,290	2,630,290
Total other debits									2,800,000	2,800,000

Example B. School district XYZ; combined statement of revenues, expenditures, and changes in fund balances; all governmental fund types and expendable trust funds, for the fiscal year ended June 30, 20XX

| | Governmental fund types | | | | Fiduciary fund type | Totals |
	General revenue	Special service	Debt projects	Capital trust	Expendable	(memorandum only)
Revenues:						
Local sources:						
Taxes	$1,016,660	$238,000	$110,000			$1,364,660
Tuition	17,440					17,440
Earnings on investments	2,200	1,000	17,84	$42,050	200	63,290
Textbook rental	9,250					9,250
	1,045,550	239,000	127,840	42,050	200	1,454,640
State sources:						
Unrestricted grants-in-aid	413,000					413,000
Restricted grants-in-aid	30,000	2,400	14,000			46,400
	443,000	2,400	14,000			459,400
Federal sources:						
Unrestricted grants-in-aid	8,900					8,900
Restricted grants-in-aid	100,000	19,000				119,000
	108,900	19,000				127,900
Total revenues	1,597,450	260,400	141,840	42,050	200	2,041,940

Example B. Continued.

	Governmental fund types				Fiduciary fund type	Totals (memorandum only)
	General revenue	Special service	Debt projects	Capital trust	Expendable	
Expenditures:						
Instruction services:						
Regular education programs	680,590	19,010				699,600
Special programs	134,200	161,230				295,430
Vocational education programs	86,270					86,270
Other instructional programs	42,090					42,090
Nonpublic school programs	1,290	4,760				6,050
Adult/continuing education programs	10,430					10,430
Community services program	3,710					3,710
	958,580	185,000				1,143,580
Support services:						
Student	78,500	14,800				93,300
Instructional staff	51,350	9,200				60,550
General administration	52,100	18,000				70,100
School administration	141,980					141,980
Business	19,970					19,970
Operation and maintenance of plant	169,080					169,080
Student transportation	17,250					17,250
Central	10,840					10,840
Other	46,820					46,820
	587,890	42,000				629,890

BUDGET PLANNING DOCUMENT - FY01

TO: PRINCIPALS AND SUPERVISORS   RETURN ENCLOSED DOCUMENTS
ON 28 FEBRUARY 2001 IN DUPLICATE

FROM: TO: _____

RE: BUDGET PLANNING -FY01   FROM: _____SCHOOL/DEPT.

DATE: DECEMBER, 2000   _____PRINCIPAL
OR SUPERVISOR

THE PURPOSE OF THE BUDGET PLANNING DOCUMENT IS TO ESTABLISH THE
NEEDS OF SCHOOLS BASED ON PROJECTED ENROLLMENT AND ADOPTED
SCHOOL GOALS. THE ALLOWABLE BUDGET ALLOCATIONS LISTED ARE TENTATIVE
TARGETS AND WILL BE ADJUSTED ONCE BUDGET APPROVAL IS RECEIVED.

****

SCHOOL BUDGET ALLOCATIONS	FY01	FY02	FY03
#242 TRAVEL	$	$	$____
#274 FIELD TRIPS	$	$	____
#289 STAFF DEVELOPMENT	$	$	____
#225 OFFICE SUPPLIES/EQUIPMENT	$	$	____
#227 TEXTBOOKS/SUPPLEMENTAL BKS.	$	$	____
#222 LIBRARY BKS/SUPPLIES	$	$	____
#223 AUDIO VISUAL SUPPLIES	$	$	____
#221 INSTRUCTIONAL SUPPLIES	$	$	____
#221 ATHLETIC SUPPLIES	$	$	____
#213 MEDICAL SUPPLIES	$	$	____
#26C MAINTENANCE SUPPLIES	$	$	____

****

DISTRICT BUDGET ALLOCATIONS	FY01
#232 SUPERINTENDENTS	____
#121 CURRICULUM SUPERVISOR (READING/ART/SOCIAL STUDIES)	____
#152 CURRICULUM SUPERVISOR (MATH/SCIENCE)	____
#17B EXCEPTIONAL CHILDREN DIRECTOR	____
#232 STUDENT SERVICES DIRECTOR	____
#288 INFORMATION SVCS. TECHNOLOGY/MEDIA	____
#285 TESTING COORDINATOR	____
#310 SCHOOL FOOD SERVICES DIRECTOR	____
#261 BUILDING & GROUNDS DIRECTOR	____
#251 BUDGET OFFICER	____

(REMINDER: SUPERVISORS SHOULD COORDINATE SPECIAL AREA PROGRAM
NEEDS WITH THE SCHOOL PRINCIPALS.)

(NOTE: SUPERVISOR BUDGETS ARE CENTRALLY FUNDED; THEREFORE,
DOLLARS WILL NOT BE GIVEN AS A TOTAL BUDGET TARGET. PLEASE SUBMIT
YOUR ANNUAL NEEDS.)

PAGE
BUDGET PLANNING DOCUMENT-FY01

IN ORDER TO PREPARE THE BUDGET DOCUMENT FOR FY01, YOUR REQUESTS
AND NEEDS MUST BE SUBMITTED IN TWO (2) COPIES NO LATER THAN 28
FEBRUARY 2001. PLEASE UTILIZE THIS COVER LETTER IN YOUR SUBMISSION.
AFTER RECEIVING YOUR BUDGET REQUESTS, A REVIEW SCHEDULE WILL BE
ESTABLISHED IN MID-MARCH 2000. PRESENTATION OF THE FY01 BUDGET
DOCUMENT WILL BE MADE TO THE SCHOOL BOARD AT A SERIES OF MEETINGS
IN MAY/JUNE 2000.

****

SCHOOL/DEPARTMENT: _____

PERSONNEL PROJECTIONS

INSTRUCTIONAL SERVICES	2001/2002	2002/2003	INCREASE/DECREASE
#110 EARLY CHILDHOOD			
#120 KINDERGARTEN			
#131 GRADE 1			
#132 GRADE 2			
#133 GRADE 3			
#134 GRADE 4			
#135 GRADE 5			
#136 GRADE 6			
#137 GRADE 7			
#138 GRADE 8			

NON-GRADED, PK-GR 8:

#141 ART			
#142 MUSIC/BAND			
#143 PE/HEALTH			
#144 READING			
#146 FOREIGN LANGUAGE			
#147 COMMUNICATION SKILLS RESOURCES			
#147 SOCIAL STUDIES			
#148 SCIENCE			
#148 SCIENCE RESOURCE			
#149 ASSESSMENT RESOURCE			

NON-GRADED, GRADE 9-12:

#144 READING			
#151 ENGLISH/LANGUAGE			
#152 MATHEMATICS			
#153 SCIENCE			
#154 SOCIAL STUDIES			
#155 FOREIGN LANGUAGE			
#156 FINE ARTS (ART)			
#156 FINE ARTS (MUSIC			
#157 PHYSICAL EDUCATION			
#157 HEALTH			

PAGE
BUDGET PLANNING DOCUMENT-FY01

INSTRUCTIONAL SERVICES	2001/2002	2002/2003	INCREASE/DECREASE
#161 BUSINESS			
#162 INDUSTRIAL ARTS			
#163 HOME ECONOMICS			

SPECIAL INSTRUCTIONAL PROGRAMS

	2001/2002	2002/2003	INCREASE/DECREASE
#171 HEARING/SPEECH/ VISUAL IMPAIRED			
#172 GIFTED/TALENTED			
#173 ENGLISH AS 2ND LANGUAGE			
#174 SP ED/LEARNING DISABLED/SPECIFIC LEARNING DISABILITY			
#174 SP ED/LANGUAGE LEARNING DISABILITY			
#174 SP ED/SELF CONTAINED SPECIFIC LEARNING DISABILITY			
#175 SP ED/PRESCHOOL HANDICAP			
#176 SP ED/PHYSICAL HANDICAP			
#177 SP ED/BEHAVIORAL EMOTIONAL HANDICAP			
#178 OCCUPATIONAL THERAPIST			
#178 PHYSICAL THERAPIST			
#179 SP ED/CROSS CATEGORICAL			
#179 SP ED/MULTIPLE HANDICAP			
#179 SP ED/ARTISTIC			
#179 SP ED/INCLUSION			
#179 SP ED/EMOTIONAL/ MENTALLY HANDICAP			
#17B SP ED/RESOURCE TMH/SPH			

OTHER INSTRUCTIONAL PERSONNEL

	2001/2002	2002/2003	INCREASE/DECREASE
#196 EDUCATIONAL AID -OA (IA)			
#196 EDUCATIONAL AID- OA (PA)			
#196 ED. AID-OA-CAI LAB (IA)			

PAGE
BUDGET PLANNING DOCUMENT-FY01

SUPPORT PERSONNEL POSITIONS

	2001/2002	2002/2003	INCREASE/DECREASE

(SUPPORT-STUDENT SERVICES)

#211 SOCIAL WORKER			
#212 GUIDANCE			
#213 HEALTH-NURSE			
#214 PSYCHOLOGICAL			

INSTRUCTIONAL SERVICES

(SUPPORT SERVICES-INSTRUCTIONAL STAFF)

#222 MEDIA COORDINATOR			
#222 LIBRARY TECHNICIANS			

(SUPPORT SERVICES-GENERAL ADMINISTRATION)

#232 SUPERINTENDENT			
#232 ASSOCIATE SUPT/INST.			
#232 ASSISTANT SUPT/FINANCE			
#232 SUPV/CURRICULUM (MATH/SCIENCE)			
#232 SUPV/CURRICULUM (READING/ART/SOC. STUDIES)			
#232 SUPV/EXCEPTIONAL CHILDREN PROGRAM			
#232 SUPV/STUDENT SERVICES			
#232 SUPV/TECHNOLOGY			
#232 OFFICE SVCS CLK (RECP)			
#232 SECRETARIES STENO			
#232 PERSONNEL CLERK			
#234 EVALUATORS			

(SUPPORT SERVICES-SCHOOL ADMINISTRATION)

#241 SCHOOL PRINCIPAL			
#241 ASSISTANT PRINCIPAL			
#242 SCHOOL SECRETARIES			
#242 OFFICE AO/ECAMS			
#261 BLDG. CUSTODIAN			

PAGE
BUDGET PLANNING DOCUMENT-FY01

(SUPPORT SERVICES-BUSINESS)

	2001/2002	2002/2003	INCREASE/DECREASE
#251 BUDGET OFFICER	_____	_____	_____
#251 PAYROLL TECHNICIANS	_____	_____	_____
#252 BUDGET ASSISTANTS	_____	_____	_____
#252 BUDGET CLERK	_____	_____	_____
#252 PROPERTY ACCTING CLK	_____	_____	_____
#253 SUPPLY TECHNICIANS	_____	_____	_____
#253 MATERIALS HANDLER	_____	_____	_____
#253 MESSENGER	_____	_____	_____
#254 OFFSET PRESS OPERATOR	_____	_____	_____

SUPPORT PERSONNEL POSITIONS

(SUPPORT PERSONNEL POSITIONS)

	2001/2002	2002/2003	INCREASE/DECREASE
#261 BLDG/GROUNDS DIRECTOR	_____	_____	_____
#261 MAINTENANCE	_____	_____	_____
#261 GARDENER	_____	_____	_____
#261 CUSTODIAL WORKER	_____	_____	_____

(SUPPORT SERVICES - CENTRAL)

	2001/2002	2002/2003	INCREASE/DECREASE
#284 COMPUTER SPECIALIST	_____	_____	_____
#284 OFFICE AUTO CLERK	_____	_____	_____
#284 MEDIA CLERK	_____	_____	_____
#284 COMMUNITY RELATIONS COORDINATOR	_____	_____	_____

(FOOD SERVICES OPERATIONS)

	2001/2002	2002/2003	INCREASE/DECREASE
#310 FOOD SVCS DIRECTOR	_____	_____	_____
#310 CAFETERIA MANAGER	_____	_____	_____
#310 ACCOUNTING TECHNICIAN	_____	_____	_____
#310 OA-CASH CLERKS	_____	_____	_____

Index

accountability programs, 20
accounting, 69–70; business, 69;
    double-entry system, 70;
    financial, 70; public school, 69;
    trial balance sheet, 72–74
Advisory Commission on
    Intergovernmental Relations
    (ACIR), 51, 52, 53
American Institute of Certified
    Public Accountants (AICPA), 69,
    82
Annan, Kofi, 6
annual financial report, 77
assessed value, 46
audits, 78–79; economy, 79;
    efficiency, 79; performance, 79;
    program, 79

balance sheet, trial, 72–74
behaviors, high-risk, 10
bilingual education, 17, 50
Bill of Rights, 47
bonded indebtedness, 87, 92
budgets, 65–82; administration, 75;
    report, 75; school-level, 66
building reserve funds, 87
busing, 17

capital outlay expenditures, 85–86
Center for Disease Control, 10
charter schools
child nutritional programs, 50
combination/tier programs, 39
Constitution, 47, 48
construction, 89–90
courts, state, 55; appellate, 55;
    general jurisdiction, 55;
    intermediate appellate, 55; small
    claims, 55; special jurisdiction,
    55; supreme, 55
Cumberland Co, N.C., 75
current revenues, 86

decentralized system, 45
disabilities, 17
district power-equalizing plan, 40
division of labor, 1
downsizing, 4

economic growth, 1
educational adequacy, 17, 26, 58
Education for the Disadvantaged,
    48
Education for the Handicapped, 48
education expenditures, 18

About the Author

Enid Beverley Jones is an associate professor in the doctoral and masters programs in Educational Leadership at Fayetteville State University in North Carolina. Her degrees include a B.S. (Economics) from the University of the West Indies; and MBA (Finance) from New York University, NY; and the Ed.D. (Educational Leadership) from the University of Florida in Gainesville, FL.

In her current position, Dr. Jones performs a multitude of functions, including serving as director for the doctoral program in Education; as member of School Superintendent Advisory Panel for Education Testing Service; project director for several grants from public and private funding agencies; proposal reader for federal, state and local government agencies, member of City Commission, and as advisor to the public school system.

Her publications include journal articles on school finance inequities–both inter-district and intra-district, issues of special education funding; and the use of technology in school administration. She has made several presentations national and state conferences on school finance and related issues such as: *Budget Priorities of Selected Principals* and *The Odds Tracing the Cost of Inclusion.* Dr. Jones is a member of several professional organizations, including the American Education Finance, Association, American Association for Research in Education, and the North Carolina Association for Research in Education.